So Good

IT HURTS...

the pain. the fight. the love.

So Good
IT HURTS...

the pain. the fight. the love.

Na'Kisha Crawford, M.Ed.

PATHWAY PUBLISHING
RANCHO CUCAMONGA, CA

Pathway Publishing
7201 Archibald Ave Suite 4-120
Rancho Cucamonga, CA 91701

Copyright © 2008 by Na'Kisha Crawford

All Rights Reserved. This book may not be reproduced in whole or in part, stored in a retrieval system, or transmitted in any form or by any means electronic, mechanical, or other without written permission from the publisher, except by a reviewer, who may quote brief passages in a review.

Cover & Interior Design: Irene Archer
www.book-cover-design.com

Edited by: Michael McIrvin
www.a-1writingandediting.writernetwork.com

Publisher's Cataloging-in-Publication
(Provided by Quality Books, Inc.)

Crawford, Na'Kisha.
So Good It Hurts: The Pain. The Fight. The Love./
Na'Kisha Crawford
p. cm.
LCCN 2008924194
ISBN-13: 978-0-9744769-1-9
ISBN-10: 0-9744769-1-9

1. Self-actualization (Psychology) 2. Man-woman relationships. 3. Love. I. Title.

BF637.S4C73 2008   158.1
QBI08-600101

Dedication

I dedicate this book to LaRon Jr. (LJ), Ndiah (Nd) and Samiyah. One day, you will understand this and it won't be a day too soon. Some things in life will cause you **pain**. Sometimes, those things are worth the **fight** but nothing in life matters without **love**.

Contents

PART ONE — PAIN 1

CHAPTER ONE—Definition of a Man 3
   Real Talk 1 9
CHAPTER TWO—Playing with Fire 11
   Real Talk 2 15
CHAPTER THREE—Freakin' and Creepin' 17
   Real Talk 3 26
CHAPTER FOUR—Love Don't Live Here 27
   Real Talk 4 33
CHAPTER FIVE—Closure Conversation 35
   Real Talk 5 42
CHAPTER SIX—Pregnant by Who? 43
   Real Talk 6 52
CHAPTER SEVEN—Making it Through 53
   Real Talk 7 64

PART TWO — FIGHT 67

CHAPTER EIGHT—Prize or Not? 69
   Real Talk 8 79
CHAPTER NINE—Baby Momma Drama 81
   Real Talk 9 92
CHAPTER TEN—Resilient but Human 93
   Real Talk 10 105
CHAPTER ELEVEN—Checklist 107
   Real Talk 11 115
CHAPTER TWELVE—Why NOT Me? 117
   Real Talk 12 123

PART THREE – LOVE 125

CHAPTER THIRTEEN—Music was My First Love 127
   Real Talk 13 129
CHAPTER FOURTEEN—Get it Together............ 131
   Real Talk 14 138
CHAPTER FIFTEEN—Have Enough to Give 139
   Real Talk 15 146
CHAPTER SIXTEEN—Forgive but Never Forget 147
   Real Talk 16 159
CHAPTER SEVENTEEN—You Don't Know Me 161
   Real Talk 17 165
CHAPTER EIGHTEEN—In the Meantime........... 167
   Real Talk 18 173

Acknowledgements

I would like to first thank my Heavenly Father for bringing my heart around to meet with my vision once again for the creation of this project. God is So Real.

To my husband, Mr. LaRon Hall, for opening up your heart to my life and everything that I am. I appreciate your love and support. Thank you for being strong enough to go through the pain, the fight and the love with me when all was said and done and for being open enough to share it. To my beautiful LJ and Nd, you took the most from me over these past few years but you have given me the most in return. I love you.

Mom and Dad, I love you both so much and I hope that I am a reflection of all that is good in both of you. Mom, Mrs. Glory Ann Williams, I lived much of my love experience through your eyes even when your heart wouldn't allow you to tell me. Dad, Mr. Albert Lee Crawford, I lived much of my love experience through your heart even when your eyes wouldn't allow you to tell me. Now, my eyes and my heart are sharing it with the world as I live it for myself.

To my family, my brothers and sisters, aunts and uncles, cousins, niece and nephews; your struggle has been my fight. I want to acknowledge you all because I love you and I want love for each of you. Don't give up in the pain. Determine that you are reason enough to fight. Win in the love that you are all so deserving of.

And to my grandmother, Nora Mae Jones, I will always keep a piece of your love with me.

To a few of my girls/personal editors, those of you who took the time to read my book and provide me with your feedback before it was a hit, I was listening. Sherri Anderson, Tracy Brown, Sheree Hoggro, Elisha Jackson, Imetra "Candy" Joiner, Stephanie Rankins, Demetria Titus and Chana West, I thank you guys and I appreciate you and to my cousin Shawana Walker, thanks for your excitement at the halfway mark. To my best girlfriends, I love you guys. And to my sorors of Delta Sigma Theta Sorority, Inc., Eta Omega Chapter of San Jose State University and Six Degrees of Determination Spring 95, Oo-Oop! You are fantastic examples of womanhood.

To those of you that have believed in me over the years, the ones who I have motivated, I thank you. You are the reason I have remained inspired to give the world a piece of me. I appreciate the support of all of you who took part in the *Real Talk on Love N Relationships* project. Thanks for fueling the fire. To those young men and women that need my inspiration, I got you. Never give up in the pain or the fight because love is waiting on the other side.

To those of you who helped me bring another vision into reality, I thank you. This is my dream now watch it grow.

Lastly, I would like to give a special Thank You to Lynn Clemmons, Veronica Clinkscales, Tiffany Gilbert, Forrest D.L. Hightower, and Darlene Miles because you cared enough when times were the hardest...

"This book describes both a struggle and an overcoming"
—IMETRA JOINER, 45, TEACHER

"A powerful display of resilience; Thought –provoking and reassuring with all of the struggles that the author goes through, still coming out on the other side maybe I can too."
—CHANA D. WEST, 28
SR. CLINICAL MEASUREMENT ANALYST

"In a book about love and relationships, I'm looking for someone with experience to give me insight on what love really is, the ups and the downs and I strongly feel that this book does that."
—STEPHANIE RANKINS, 25
FINANCIAL OPERATIONS ASSISTANT

"We all have things to endure and it's sometimes so easy for people outside of the story to observe and judge. It's so easy to do and this book is a reminder that each person has to make their own decision about who and why to love."
—DEMETRIA TITUS, 32, ATTORNEY

"The dating world is exhausting and unfulfilling and although I do believe in true love, it may not be granted to everyone for various reasons. The one commonality however is that we all want hope and this book provides it."
—SHEREE HOGGRO, 32, REAL ESTATE BROKER

Never allow someone to be your priority while allowing yourself to be their option.

—Author Unknown

Introduction

Relationship issues that arise between men and women have gotten many of us to a point of despair, and loneliness has led us to do things that we are not so proud of. Because I have been there on both counts, my hope is that, by honestly sharing my experiences, the misery some of you suffer might be soothed. I have been so disappointed in myself and in love that I wished someone was there to tell me that I wasn't the only one or that it would get better. That's right, dear reader: even smart and beautiful women like you experience drama in relationships, and this book will take your mind off of your own love struggle for a while and give you ideas for moving forward to a better you, with or without your current relationship. In few words, *So Good It Hurts* is the good, the bad, and the sometimes ugly truth about love and relationships.

This book provides the "real talk" necessary when we know what we need to do but just can't seem to muster up the courage to let him go. This book will touch on the sometimes embarrassing truths that hurt so bad that we inadvertently ask for more by prolonging the inevitable. We stay in relationships that are stagnant, with men who will not commit to us or with those who have no respect for us, but we are hopeful. We give to partners who only take. We want to grow with people who aren't growing. Nothing in this book is new, and in fact I would guess that much of what you will read is but the echo of a voice from deep down inside you that has told you the same things. Likewise, you could ask any older woman or man about some of the challenges they have faced over the years in relationships, and you would hear many of the same stories you are about to read. However, the core values that have contributed to strong and lasting relationships in the past seem to have been forgotten by the younger generations, and so this book will serve as a reminder.

I remember feeling pain so deep that I didn't think I would be able to move forward. Deep inside, the source of that little voice I mentioned earlier, I was mature enough to know that I would get through it, but I felt like I couldn't at the time and my feelings were what mattered. I knew that both the love and the pain were real. I couldn't write them off as just part of being in my early twenties or because I wasn't in a committed relationship or marriage and so the feeling should not count. I couldn't ignore the feelings because he was in a relationship with other women as well as with me, and that really struck a nerve. I must admit, however, and I had to admit it even then, that much of that pain was self inflicted. In many instances, I allowed these situations to go forth. I wasn't strong enough. I wasn't good enough. I couldn't make him love me enough to give me what I wanted. These negative thoughts were all temporary though. I soon figured out that I wasn't strong enough because I didn't believe that I was strong, and I believed I wasn't good enough because I didn't accept that I was better than the treatment I was allowing. It might be surprising to hear, but I always knew in my heart, the source of that voice again, that I was better, even stronger, and yet I couldn't keep bad relationship scenarios from becoming my reality. There are two people in a relationship, and it is important to keep in mind that other people's weaknesses or faults are not about you. Sometimes, he's just not the right man, or perhaps you are not the right woman. The failing relationship might just be bad timing for both of you. The important point to remember is that you have to get yourself right so that you are ready to take on your next worthy relationship with confidence and poise.

I have written about this topic, love and relationships, because I fear that as a society we are heading in the wrong direction when it comes to what is acceptable. I know that I may be a bit hopeful, even idealistic perhaps, to think that relationships can work out and are necessary for the majority of us to be happy, successful, and fulfilled in our lives. However, I believe that strong relationships are important for our children and important for us as adults. In order to really make a relationship work, we need to believe in and support the concept of a strong family base. That base begins with two healthy individuals, and although I have accepted that issues between these adults will create a little character and strength, relationships today need to be stronger and healthier. In fact, it seems that we are too quick to give up on anything even slightly challenging, and indeed we need to invest some time and effort in a relationship. However, often times, we are dealing with people who are not healthy from the start, and instead of confronting issues, we try to build a relationship on top of the issues. Anything built on a weak foundation is likely to be short-lived and unhealthy. I am writing this book because I believe that God is love and that, through God, we too will each find love. We have to move past the temporary feelings and believe in, and hope for, love.

Part One
the Pain

CHAPTER ONE
Definition of a Man

I never looked at him as a potential relationship partner before, even though he had been flirting and showing signs of interest in me for quite some time. One reason I had not considered him before was because he started at State a couple of years after I did, and therefore, I figured he was a little younger than I was. At the time, it wasn't so popular to date younger men, unless of course the woman was old enough to teach him a few things. Another reason that I had not considered him in this way was because I was waiting on something, or should I say that I was waiting on someone with whom a relationship worth my energy was never going to happen.

When I started college, I had a boyfriend from high school. My father told me that it wasn't a good idea to go to college with a boyfriend, especially one who was not also in college. I only knew that my high school sweetheart and I loved each other and he was there for me, and so I asked myself, "Why shouldn't we be together?" We had been involved nearly three years by the time I started State, but little did I know that my dad's prediction would come true. I soon ended my first significant relationship, and as a seventeen year-old college freshman, I was sure that I knew all of the answers, especially about men.

I was still young and inexperienced, at least I knew that much, and so I wasn't looking for a husband yet, but I did want to broaden my horizons a bit, and I knew what I wanted in a man. Although my first boyfriend was a genuinely good guy with a few of the physical characteristics that I liked, I was more attracted to him because he was a good person and not necessarily because of how he looked. I stand 5' 7" and so I liked taller guys, at least 6'. I'll never forget a childhood friend of mine who said that she liked short guys so that they could look up to her, but as far as I was concerned, her rationale was all backward ("but hey, whatever floats your boat," I used to tell her).

At the time, I wanted men to look a certain way, dress a certain way, and act in a certain manner; but I have since learned that all I was doing was limiting my options. The more decisions I made about what this man should be like, the smaller the box I left for any man with whom I might have a relationship to exist in and the smaller the field became. I was not alone in this habit, however, far from it. Many women decrease the size of the box that their ideal mate could fit into, and then they wonder why they can't find him, why they are still alone. I was lucky. At a relatively early age, I figured out that limited thinking limits your options, and therefore, I had to make a few changes as to who my ideal man was going to be.

Of course, everything that I knew about what it means to be a woman, about men, and about relationships

DEFINITION OF A MAN

stemmed from my exposure to my parents and my extended family; and trust me, we will talk about the impact they had on me later. I'm sure society had some influence on the type of guy I liked as well, as I found myself attracted to something of a "bad boy." After all, the cliché "good girls like bad boys" came from somewhere, and every cliché has some basis in truth or it would not have survived long enough to become a cliché.

I grew up in the 80s and 90s, and the popularity of the bad boy image was at an all-time high, which meant that there was something utterly attractive to me about a guy wearing a baseball cap, loose-fitting jeans, and tennis shoes — a tough guy. Why women have this thing about shoes, I don't know, but from a very young age, my man would have to have on a decent pair. Lots of women share in this ideal about men's shoes, and as strange as it sounds, shoes might be the only reason a man can walk on by without giving him a second look.

Back to the type of man that I wanted at seventeen: he needed to be cool, and I mean the term as in calm and collected, a desire I came by honestly because my father was "Mr. Cool." I tended to like a guy who was kind of cocky and smart, but he had to have some street smarts as well, and that's where the "bad boy" ideal came into play. A man who could not handle his own, stand up for himself *and me*, would not get a chance. If this brutal honesty about what I called a man at the time makes some of you uncomfortable, remember that I am sharing my experiences and my thoughts, however naïve they may have been, so that others might be able to identify their own limitations in their choice of an ideal partner.

At the time, I firmly adhered to this simple set of requirements, and I must admit that I knew lots of guys who fit into the category. There were quite a few other characteristics that they shared that were not so good. Many of them were "players," or womanizers, for example. These guys had little respect for women, who were simply their prey, and they were more concerned about impressing their friends than they were with impressing women — they had no intention of being in a committed relationship. I mentioned that I grew up during the 80s and 90s, and if you are familiar with that time period, you may recognize it as a time when explicitly derogatory song lyrics about women were increasingly acceptable. Do I blame the music for the lack of respect that many of the young men were beginning to display? Of course not, but I do think the music had an impact, and it still does today.

I have to be honest and admit that I did recognize the signs a man was a player in most instances, but I made the same mistake many women make in thinking that I could change them. Most men change when they are ready to change. A man will not change just because you want him to, and in fact, he may decide not to change precisely because you want him to so desperately.

For the first couple of years following the end of my first significant relationship, I chose this same type of guy. He would meet my exterior expectations, but then there was a whole can of worms yet to open. I was so busy worrying about what I wanted my man to look and act like that I hadn't spent much time thinking about how he should treat me or what he should be like beyond superficial appearances. I later realized that my high school boyfriend was a treat compared to what was out there, and for that, I really do hold him in high regard still today. I had not taken the time to analyze who I was so that I'd recognize what I wanted when it finally did come along. A few rotten apples had convinced me that I had better decide what qualities my ideal man should have, and I seized on the opportunity to come up with a mental image with little depth to it.

It would be nice if I could tell you that it was overnight I discovered entirely who I was and that led directly to the formation of my definition of a man. The truth is I'm still working on me, and as for my definition of a man, well that definition started back then and has been evolving since. It would be a few more years before I'd stop trying to make things happen on my timeline though. When your heart is in the right place and you are trusting in God's timing versus your own, life will be much easier for you. Many of us are under the misconception that, if we do all that we can to meet that certain man's needs, he will be there to meet ours. Unfortunately, this is just not so. We cannot make another person see something in us that they cannot see in themselves, or more importantly, that we don't see in ourselves.

If you are trying to find that person to share the rest of your life with, or even someone to grow with for now, the last thing you want to hear is what follows, but listen up! God is sometimes working on your heart, helping you to love you, before he allows another person in. I know someone has probably told you this before, and the person who said it was probably older or married, right? I know, such a thing is easy for them to say, but the truth is, someone who has been-there and done-that often does understand where you are and that there are no easy answers. When you are longing for someone to love and share your world with, you have to trust that God knows better than you do where you are and how much you can take. Once you make the decision to define your man, be sure that you have defined who YOU are AT THAT TIME (because your definition will indeed change).

REAL TALK 1

Girl, get this through your head! First and foremost, you CAN NOT change a man. He has to change for himself, and he will do that when and only when HE is ready. Most of us make the mistake of thinking that, if we just hang in there, he will come around and give us what we want. We might even think that he'll just begin to do the right thing one day when we least expect it, and this is where we are wrong. He usually keeps doing what we allow him to get away with and he will only change if and when he wants to.

CHAPTER TWO
Playing with Fire

My second semester of college had just begun, and this time around, I knew a little something about this university thing. My first semester went well. My grades were good, and I knew my way around the campus. I made a few friends, but not many, which was surprising to me because I was always pretty social. My next door neighbor in the dorms was a guy, and we had become good friends. I would hang out with him and his friends, and from time to time, my roommate would join us. She had been in school for a couple of years already prior to my arrival, and she had maybe three friends. She spent every weekend off campus with her "crazy" boyfriend, who did not attend State, and I hoped she learned that he was not good for her before she let him ruin her life. He did not cheat on her as far as I knew, but he was incredibly controlling and jealous, and I knew even as a freshman in college that something was wrong with that picture. Stevie Wonder could see that.

The class that I happened to be adding to my schedule this day was English 1A, and it was there that I spotted him. He was tall, handsome, and dressed perfectly in my humble estimation, *wearing the baseball cap and loose pants and all*. I decided that I needed to get his attention so that he could get my number. I was seated when he came in the door, and he chose a desk not far from mine. We exchanged a few words, and by the time we left the classroom, I knew that I wanted to get to know him better. We didn't exchange numbers that day, but a couple of weeks later, I saw him again, and this time he asked to give me a call. I was pumped up by his request, screaming with excitement when I got back to my dorm room from the Dining Commons.

I didn't have much experience with men, but there was something about him that had captured my attention. He was a football player and only a couple of years older than I was, but he was obviously quite a few years more experienced than I was and I thought I could handle it. The ride was fun while it lasted, but I definitely got firsthand experience with a "player." He wasn't all that clever in his maneuvers, but then again, I was easy to fool and blinded by my attraction to his physical appearance. I had come from a line of players, and I had seen the worst kind of games being run on women by the men in my own family, including my father, and so I knew the games. Unfortunately, knowing the games didn't make me exempt from falling for them.

I tried to play for a while because I wasn't doing anything else as far as relationships went. I didn't really like anyone else at the time, and in fact, I didn't have anyone in my life. After close to a year with this womanizer, I even knew that he wasn't going to give me the type of relationship that I wanted, and therefore, I accepted the type of relationship that *he* wanted. I allowed myself to think that it was okay to remain involved with him on a physical level, even knowing that he was involved with other women, until I moved on to some deeper relationship.

I would call him from time to time in hopes that he would drop by, and other times he would call me. I wasn't really aware of the emotional connection I had to him, the emotions I thought I could put aside to continue a physical relationship and keep him in my life. He and I had become friends, but who was I fooling? I was now playing the part of the fool because I allowed this man to sleep with me even though I knew that he was sleeping with other girls, but mostly because I thought that I could control my feelings for him.

Women, there are exceptions to every rule, but in general, if you are having sex with a man on a continuous basis and he's pleasing you, you will grow deeper feelings for him. If a man tells you that he's not ready for a relationship and you are in the place in your life where you are ready, listen to him, accept his warning, and move on. It's a lot easier to control your feelings before they get too deep. Six months in is already too late. He will have sex with you even though he has no intention of having more than casual sex, but he is there because you let him be there.

It took a while for me to finally get out of that kitchen, but I did eventually. The trouble was that I walked right into another. This time, it was different, or so I told myself; but isn't it always different? I finally made the decision to try liking someone who liked me for a change, but the trouble was that I was so set on the type of guy that I wanted that my heart wasn't even ready to hear that perhaps he'd come in a different package. This new man used to always ask me to tutor him as he sat in study hall with the rest of the basketball players. My job was on campus through the Intramural Sports Department, and I would see this guy often, but I never took him seriously.

He would flirt with me and compliment me from time to time, and I must admit that it was flattering, but I was so caught up in my own drama that I didn't even think twice about him. We would see each other around campus and at social functions, but he did not seriously approach me until a year and a half after we first had contact. In the meantime, he was no longer required to go to study hall to keep his basketball scholarship. He joined a fraternity on campus, definitely increasing his rank on my desirability scale, and he had become one of State's most popular male students. Initially, I had no idea how popular, but I would soon find out.

REAL TALK 2

Girl, I know you think your getting what you want out of the arrangement, but most of the time, you are only selling yourself short when you allow a man to have casual sex with you when you know that he's also sexing other women. You already know this, but you tell yourself that you are going to get yours, what you truly deserve, and that he will change. Ha! In most cases, **PLAYED** is all you are getting. As I mentioned earlier, if he is pleasing you physically, you will fall in deeper for him, and the deeper you fall, the more your emotions will allow you to believe that he feels the same way. For him, most of the time, it's just good sex. There are exceptions to every rule, but again, when you play with fire, you will get burned.

CHAPTER THREE
Freakin' and Creepin'

We were at a fraternity social event on campus, and a few of my sorority sisters and I had gotten together that night to celebrate one of their birthdays. We had gone out to dinner and decided to go by the "Social" afterwards. There were lots of people already having a good time at the event. I don't know what made tonight different, but after all of that flirting, the basketball player finally decided to ask me out. It was the cutest thing. He gave me a hug, as we tend to do when we greet one another in the world of fraternities and sororities. My girls and I had been hanging out at this event, and he came over to me and asked me if I would like to go to the movies the next day. It happened to be a Thursday night, which worked out perfectly.

I couldn't help giggling at how cute it was that he appeared to be nervous when he asked me out. He looked so innocent and so sincere. Because he had sent the message through my sister, who was also attending State, as well as my best friend, who happened to be his sorority sister, it was really no surprise that he would get around to asking me out eventually. I had decided only weeks before that I was going to try liking someone who liked me, and this seemed like the perfect opportunity. They say that sometimes there are signs in relationships, but the fact that the movie *Thin Line Between Love and Hate* starring Martin Lawrence was the film we saw on our first date didn't ring a bell at all, at least not at that point.

We started off as friends. He was really into me in the beginning, calling me at least every other day, coming by to visit me, and even trying to support me in the many things I had going on at the time, like graduating from college for example. I had an internship, a job, and a full course load. He gave me lots of attention, and in fact, he seemed to be doing all of the right things — and boy was such treatment right on time.

However, I had still gotten a few calls from the first guy I was seeing, the player, but he just sort of faded out of my life eventually. One day I got a phone call from him though while my new friend was at my house, which was a little awkward for me, but primarily because I wasn't sure if I had a reason to finally cut Man #1 off completely. It was still too early in the second relationship to decide, and besides, I wasn't so sure I was over him. Because I am trying to be as honest as I can be, I must admit that I didn't want to hurt my new friend's feelings, but I also didn't know how to stand up to the last guy who had been able to have his way with me. I guess something in my heart was still holding on just in case he came to his senses and became a one-woman man, mine, even though it had technically been over for a couple of years. So many times in relationships, we cut ourselves the shorter end of the stick because we are looking for the man in question to validate who we are in the relationship and let us know that we are worthy, but the question remains: Is he worth it?

I thought that I learned a little something from the past few "semi-relationships" that I was involved in (those between these two relationships), so this time I tried to do a few things differently. I didn't ask any questions, and I really wasn't all that interested in the couple of ex-girlfriends that I had heard about over the past year or so. I didn't want to catch myself up in any drama, just go along for the ride until we hit a corner. Our friendship was blossoming, and although I didn't think that I would be interested in anything more than friendship with him, I started liking the company of this friend who also liked *my company*.

We had decided to take our relationship to a physical level, and as you might guess, feelings then grew stronger between us. The two of us were spending a lot of time together, and we were really getting to know each other well. He was fun and funny, and he was sensitive to my needs but strong. He was helpful and supportive, and he had the most innocent eyes. Around campus, everybody thought he was cool. He knew everyone and everyone knew him, and because I had not asked, he had not offered any information about all of the girls on campus who knew him really well. My bad! I should have asked.

This guy was apparently really impressed with me, however. I'll never forget the night he told me about this discussion group that he and a few of his friends had planned for the students when he was living on campus.

I happened to attend that night because the topics had to do with relationships and I couldn't miss the opportunity to put my two cents in. I believe "Freakin and Creepin" was the topic of the discussion, so you know the discussion was good. I gave my opinion, which I don't have a problem doing, and he interpreted that presentation, and my character as a woman, as confidence and fearlessness. He decided that night that I was the perfect blend of beauty, brains, and feistiness (his exact words).

I was graduating by this time, and he had only been in school for two years. I wasn't planning on moving away just yet, however, and in fact, I didn't know what I was going to do. I was only 21, and I had gotten off to a pretty good start in this town. I hadn't thought about a long-term relationship with my friend, but it was time to consider whether we would remain "special" friends over the summer while he moved back home to Los Angeles. He wrote me cute little notes and poems, and he bought the cutest little necklace for my graduation, something to remember him by, and so I couldn't pass up the opportunity to keep in touch.

Lots had happened over the summer, including my move to my new apartment with my best girlfriend. My friend and I wrote each other and talked on the phone, and he showed a couple of pictures of me to his father. He was excited to tell me that his dad said that I was a "keeper," and I was pleased by the compliment. Everything was going smoothly, until one day, during a phone conversation, I asked him how many girls he was involved with. At that time, we called being involved with someone "talking to" them, so when he answered four, I

FREAKIN' AND CREEPIN'

almost fell out of my seat. All I could think was, "I am one of four women he is spending time with — what have I gotten myself into?"

Then my next thoughts were, "Okay, well I better let you go because I am not going to be one on your list of women — you have to be kidding me." We ended our conversation in a friendly manner, and I was under the impression that this would be the last time we talked, at least as special friends anyway.

Ladies, don't fool yourselves like I fooled myself. I got a call from him about three weeks later like nothing had ever been discussed, and we had a friendly conversation. He was going to be moving back for school now, but we were just regular friends because I was not going to be on the list, or so I thought. I suggest you never leave doors like this open if you really plan to take care of yourself. I said that I would not be involved with him anymore, but I didn't have enough experience to know that he would call me and act as if everything was all good. I hadn't been strong enough in my conviction, and I was caught a little off-guard. I left my heart open, and my feelings got the best of me. I'm sure many of you can relate.

When he returned to school, he found himself looking for an apartment. His plans were to room with two of his fraternity brothers, but neither of them had actually made arrangements to find an apartment before school started. I guess they thought it would be easier than it turned out to be. I should have stayed out of it, but of course, being the friend that I was, I helped him find an apartment, which just happened to be in the apartment building that I lived in. Ladies, don't ever move into the same apartment complex as someone you are dating if you are not living together. I told you that the name of the movie we saw on our first date was *Thin Line Between Love and Hate*, and this experience would indeed prove that movie to have been a sign of things to come.

Over the next year or so, I found myself in a whirlwind of emotions over this guy. He had not stopped seeing the other women that he told me about over the summer, and in fact, he was adding names to his list. I told myself that I was not going to be a part of any list, but I should have told *him* and meant it. He never once said that he was going to stop seeing them, and so he did not lie to me; but as women, we sometimes fall into the he'll-change-once-he-gets-to-know-me trap. Ladies, if you tell a guy something that you are okay with versus something that you are not willing to accept, stand by your word because he will test you. The moment that you seem tempted, or even worse, the moment you act on the temptation that you told him you would not act on, you are caught up in his trap.

My feelings for this man grew stronger and stronger. There was something about this guy that made me feel. He seemed to have a kind spirit and a loving heart, but how could he do the things to me that he was doing if that were the case? I managed to ask myself that question, but I could not answer it. I knew that I was no longer a priority for him as I had been in the beginning of the relationship. He used to be so into me, but somehow, the tables had turned. How did we get here? What did I do to make him decide that I was not the "keeper" his father described me to be? He had not said that I was no longer a keeper, but his actions spoke a thousand words, ten-thousand, a million. He maintained a relationship with me, one that would keep me holding on; but ladies, a man is only going to do what you allow him to do, and unfortunately, he may actually blame you for his bad behavior. "I told you that I wasn't ready for a committed relationship when we started." Have you ever heard that one? He will do just enough to keep you hopeful but not enough to give you much hope.

The bad thing about being involved with a man who is involved with other women is that all of the women feel protective of the man and her relationship with him. We are in such competition with each other as women that we fall right into the trap that he sets up for us. He can play both ends against the middle because he is sure that we will not talk, which keeps the truth from surfacing. That works out great for him. The negative information that we are so quick to believe about another woman keeps us all getting played. Once I found out the identity of a couple of the other girls who were also involved with my "friend," the wrath grew immensely. This is how it always seems to go: We end up being so angry at the other women for being a part of our pain but we never place the blame where it belongs. Two people are responsible for their actions in a relationship, the two willing participants, but remember that he is the one that got you involved in this mess.

I have been on both sides of this sad scenario. I didn't know that my friend was involved with other women when we started our relationship, but when I did find out, I didn't stop my relationship with him. Unfortunately, this tends to be true of all of us as well: We are often way into the guy by the time we find out the truth, and so we don't just walk away. Once we know though, if we don't walk, we are a willing participant when he starts up a new relationship with another woman who probably doesn't know. Although there are those women who could care less that this guy they are involved with is also involved with someone else, there are lots more who are completely innocent when they get involved with men who happen to be involved with others. Most of us are the latter, just getting duped.

After some time passed, I was now officially "in love." I never offered "love" quickly in any relationship, even if I thought I felt it early on, but it had been a year and I felt like my feelings were real. When I was with the first guy I was involved with in college, I used to tell myself that I loved him when I got excited about something he'd done. However, as soon as the words came out of my mouth, I'd say to myself, "No you don't! You have no reason to!" Be truthful with yourself, ladies, if you have no reason to be in love. The truth was that, although he was very nice looking and a great dresser with a tough boy attitude, he could be a real jerk sometimes. He gave me no reason to love him, and I reminded myself of that often. Women sometimes see something that does not exist because we want it so badly when, in fact, the qualities we want may not be a part of the man that we have. Don't fool yourself into seeing something that was never there in the first place.

If you've been in a relationship with a man you cared for, whether he was involved with others or not, you know that it's difficult to stop seeing him. It would be nice if the fact that he was involved with "other women" made it easier, but often, those are the toughest relationships to end. Women hate to lose to another woman, and so we stick it out, hoping to win the man even if he ain't such a "prize." But society also has us so scared about the man-to-woman ratio and so we don't think there are enough men out there. Some of us have been alone for so long that we start thinking it's better to have a piece of this man than to have no man at all.

Another reason that breaking it off with this particular guy was so difficult was that I had become friends with his circle of friends. It is so hard to cut off everybody we knew in common, but ladies, all of the women that your man is involved with are cool with his friends if you are. So you aren't all that special to them either, and you can't hang out with his friends and not ever run into him or wonder about what he's doing when he isn't around. We hate to think that "our man" is giving what we wanted and deserved to another woman, but in truth, most of the time, he's not. He's not giving them anything different than he is giving you, some small portion of his time and attention.

REAL TALK 3

Girl, if he won't give you the commitment you want, living in closer proximity to him is not going to change that. He's not going to stop what he's doing. Instead, he's just going to be a little slicker. If I have said nothing else so far that you have taken to heart, make a note of this: HE WILL DO JUST ENOUGH TO KEEP YOU HOPEFUL BUT NOT ENOUGH TO GIVE YOU MUCH HOPE.

Remember also that this competition between us, between women, only keeps us entrapped in our own pain. Whether we are jealous of each other or we want what the other woman has so that we'll feel better about ourselves, the man wins this fight, not either of us. We are so eager to believe any negative information about each other, but ask yourselves why this great man that you care so much about would be involved with a woman who is stupid and crazy and has nothing going for her. What does that say about him? Don't take your frustration out on the other woman if you won't even stand up to the man who has you involved in the triangle in the first place. What kind of sense does that make? In the words of Charlie Murphy: "We gotta do better".

Also, Just because God wants each of us to experience love doesn't mean that you have to love any and everyone, not romantically anyway. The truth is that, many times, he doesn't have much to offer you worth loving him for. Pay attention.

CHAPTER FOUR
Love Don't Live Here

Living in the same apartment building as the guy I was seeing, as you could probably imagine, opened the door to lots of communication and interaction with his roommates. It also opened the door to lots of heartache for me. We were all good friends, and that was fine, but ladies, if you are friends with his friends, remember that their loyalty is to him. In relationships, sometimes we find ourselves thinking about what we would do or how we would act, but men are men, which means, to put it mildly, they don't think like women. I speak about men being players and womanizers, but it is true that some women can be just as bad as men, using them for sex, money, and more. Some women do think similarly to men, but many of them have been hurt previously and decided to make decisions of the heart based on avoiding any more pain. I mentioned earlier that I come from a long line of players, and so let me break down in detail a little of my family experience. If you don't think that your past or family upbringing has affected your relationships, you are mistaken.

The top "Player" in my family was my maternal grandmother, a surprise revelation, I am sure. She was and still is the matriarch of my family, and with her many years of experience in love and relationships, she is what some would call a Bad Mamma Jamma. My grandmother is raw and uncut. She has always taken men with a grain of salt. As soon as one was gone, she would be on to the next. She did have her relationship rules though, and unlike any of the lessons that I am sharing throughout this book, her rules were more like, "If he can't do anything for you, you don't need him" or "If he's not paying, he's not staying." My grandmother didn't value men too much, in other words, but that stemmed from her early experiences. She didn't think very highly of her step-father, who was so mean that she did what she could to get out of the house, which in those days meant getting married and having a baby. She moved out by the time she was 16, and within the next couple of years, she was on to the next man and baby #2 was on the way. She went on to have several relationships, and although she only married twice, she had a total of nine children, three girls and six boys. She had lots of children to teach her rules to.

My grandmother did what she had to in order to take care of herself and her children. She came up during a time when education was not accessible to many African Americans, and moreover, going to school certainly wasn't going to feed children or pay bills. Being a single woman, my grandma began doing what she knew worked. She played men and got all her financial needs met. She was a social butterfly and enjoyed having a good time. She was a great catch and still thinks she's pretty damned hot today. She managed to find a few men she really cared for along the way, but that wasn't enough to keep her around. I asked my grandmother a few years back which man, of all of the men she had been in serious relationships with, really loved her? She answered me with a firm, "None of them." My heart broke for her. She went through life feeling like she had never been loved. Now I understood why her sentiment about love was that "Love Don't Live Here No More."

My family has included more players than I care to mention, however. The list ranges from incredibly charming and handsome gentlemen to dirty pimps, *and they may have been a little handsome as well.* Yes, I mean that term literally too. I had a couple of family members who were actual pimps for women who allowed themselves to be prostituted for money. I am in no way implying that the men were any better than those women because the behavior associated with the sex trade is all-around terrible for the women and the men, but these men affected more than they could have imagined by treating these women this way and by not valuing or respecting themselves or women in general.

Most of the men in my family dated several women at a time. Marriage was mostly unheard of, and the few times these people, my relatives, got married, the marriage was a joke from the beginning. The institution of marriage wasn't really valued, in short, but neither were relationships. The women in my family were even being mistreated by the men in their lives. Not all of the men in my family are "bad boys," however. There are a few good ones in the bunch, but the vast majority of them seem to be conscious of the rules that my grandmother set in place and never trusted women. It didn't take long before they would teach the younger males in my family their rules, a vicious cycle. The downside was that the girls also learned that men could be expected to mistreat women, and so, in a ridiculous kind of way, they learned the truth about relationships. However, they only learned the partial truth because they did not know that they were allowed to expect better.

In fact, many of the males in my family shared women, passed them around, and I really felt sorry for those women and can only hope that some of them have been able to pick up the pieces of their lives and move on. In a nutshell, in my family: the men had no respect for the women, the women had little respect for the men, none of them had much respect for themselves, and they all mistreated each other in the worst ways imaginable. It is probably not surprising that many of them are currently not in loving relationships or are not in healthy ones. A few have been fortunate enough to find significant others to strengthen and enrich their lives, but many of them missed the Love Boat altogether.

Since growing up, I have learned that many of my family members have been carrying pain for years. I realized that they were longing for a companion, a friend, someone who truly loved them and that this is not uncommon in most families today. They went through life thinking that they would never have a true and meaningful relationship, but once they learned that such a thing is truly possible, it was too late to try to get it right. My grandmother is getting older and would like a companion, but she is so hard and has gone so long without the kind of fulfilling love connection that should be shared between two people that she chooses to accept that she will never have true love. This absolutely breaks my heart.

An interesting part of this story of my family, and one of the reasons that I am sharing it with you, is that, although I saw the men in my family mistreat women and show little concern or respect for their feelings, they treated me and the women in my family like jewels for the most part. That may seem strange, but I discovered later that I was able to see the good in men, even the bad boys, because I always saw the good in the men in my family. They loved me. They protected me. They supported me and encouraged me, but they never made any connection between honoring me and their mistreatment of the women who were a part of *someone else's* family. I saw good guys doing bad things, and I learned that not all "bad boys" were really that bad. These men had good hearts, which could be discovered if they allowed someone to get close enough. The men in my family weren't afraid that I would misuse or hurt them. They did not fear me, and therefore, there was no need to put up a wall or a front. They could love the girls in the family without fear of judgment for loving too much or not having enough.

The effect of growing up in such a family has been double-edged. I sought a man who had experienced a few downfalls in life and made it through. I wanted someone with a tougher exterior because I knew this kind of heart. I wanted the bad boy but with the sensitivity and respect of a good man. We all seek the familiar, and although there would be some similar traits between the one I would end up with and my family members, I knew that I would not accept a man who would mistreat me the way I witnessed so many women being treated when I was a child. The men in my family, although they were guilty of such things themselves, wouldn't sit by and allow me to be misused by a man. This is all a good thing.

Coming from the line of "players" and now having the little experience that I had personally, I refused to be completely run over. I had to learn on my own though that the men I was involving myself with had no obligation to love me, and it was a tough lesson, one I had to be exposed to over and over again. This was the bad part of the effect of growing up in such a family. If only the men in my family knew that they were planting seeds that would hurt so many women and even hurt themselves, they may have made better decisions.

Now that I have explained to you where my heart was and my understanding of why my heart was there, maybe it will be easier for you to understand the upcoming difficulties that I would allow myself to face, over and over again. These challenges made me question my decisions enough times that I finally drew a few connections to my past experiences. In fact, although these were tough lessons to learn, I ask myself even today: Did I ever *really* learn them?

REAL TALK 4

My family is what it is, and I love them. I knew I wasn't crazy though, and I needed to draw a connection to prove it. I was also looking for a way out. Who could I blame for the situations I was getting myself in? Who are you trying to blame besides you and him and, occasionally, her? No matter how much we twist and turn the facts, we are responsible for our own actions or lack thereof. My past did explain a few things to me, but it didn't provide an out. I didn't jump up with an S on my chest after the discovery because I was still caught in a bad relationship with someone who wouldn't even call me his girlfriend. The real question remained: What was I going to do now that I had this information?

CHAPTER FIVE
Closure Conversation

I made up my mind not to continue in a relationship that was hurting me so badly. I would find myself wondering if he had made it home some nights, running around to the outside of his apartment to see if his bedroom light was on. I know — that really was sad. When he didn't answer the phone but I could see that the light was on, I would have a problem. It was also a problem when I went over to his house and his roommates, my friends, told me that he wasn't there. It hurt so bad to think that he was in his room with another girl just a few doors down.

Moreover, he would not give me the title of being his "girlfriend," which was what I longed for. It may seem silly, but I wanted to be his girlfriend because I wanted the commitment I thought that term entailed. It seemed that I had been caught in the semi-relationship role for too long, and I was beginning to get down on myself for allowing too much without the commitment a girlfriend should have. I backed away from the relationship several times, or at least I tried, but he would call me up as if everything was all good, as if I'd never asked him to stop calling. I would go out on dates with other guys and really try to focus my energy on other relationships, but that didn't work. I still had feelings for him. However, I found out so much information about his other relationships that I had to do something. He was involved with two of the women on his "list" for much longer than he had been involved with me. One of them lived back home in Los Angeles and was his high school girlfriend, and the other one had been involved with him since they started college, which was for about three years by the time I was approaching the year and a half mark. I remember thinking to myself, "If you're thinking about outstaying them, you should forget it."

I figured that, if I was going to be involved in a relationship that included these other girlfriends, I'd better get to know the competition if I planned on sticking it out. I didn't really think there was much to worry about from the high school girlfriend because, after all, she was several miles away and she wasn't doing much with herself. This does not mean that she was not a good person, but I just didn't see her as competition for me. However, the girl at State was willing to do *anything* for him. Perhaps I didn't have too much room to judge her in this regard, but nevertheless, that was sickening to me. She was the worst kind of woman to have on the other end when you are involved with a more-than-one-woman man. She made him her life. She believed every word he said, even over her friends. She had been pregnant by him a few times but had no children. She was willing to be the girlfriend without making him adhere to the rules of a commitment, things like not having to call before you come over and the like. She hated me with a passion,

CLOSURE CONVERSATION

and I have to admit that the feelings were reciprocated, *although we never had a single conversation*. In fact, we did exactly what he wanted by despising each other.

Over time, lots of information about such a player will always surface. When you start looking, you shall find, but this can be a good or bad thing — good if you do something with it and bad if you don't. I was never threatened much by the other women in his life because I always felt that they couldn't compare to me. My problem was with the fact that he did not see that as clearly as I did. I was confident in my qualities and knew where I stood as a young woman, but if I was so together, how could I allow myself to participate in such a cruel game? There was something wrong with this picture, and at the time I could not figure it out. I had already graduated from college, was making good money, taking care of myself, and had a nice apartment and car. I was confident in who I was, and getting attention from men was never a problem for me. I'd somehow gotten myself stuck on this one, who didn't seem to know where he wanted to go or who he wanted to take with him.

I had a conversation with him one night, telling him how much he meant to me. I asked him to please let me be because I couldn't handle what was going on with us. This was supposed to be a conversation for closure on my part, but girl, you can't have closure when your heart is wide open. He broke down his feelings for me, telling me that he loved me and how much I meant to him but that he still wasn't ready to commit. He even had the nerve to compare me with the other woman, and I could have died. He said something like, "She's pretty; you're pretty.

She's smart; you're smart." I couldn't believe my ears because I was convinced that she did not come close. I was independent, working on my Master's degree, and determined to be successful; and she was barely in school and taking his word as his bond in spite of the fact that she knew his two-timing ways better than I did. It was my opinion that she didn't compare to me, but his opinion was the one that mattered here. What should this have told me? It doesn't matter how together you are. You can get played so you had better stay on guard.

Nevertheless, after having this conversation with him, I felt like maybe one day things would be good between us. I held on to the fact that he said he loved me and I knew that he wasn't ready to let me go. In my heart, I couldn't believe that he would do some of the things that he had done to hurt me. In my heart to this day I never truly believed that he did any of what he did *to* hurt me, but the fact is his words and his behavior cut like a knife.

I remember coming home to my apartment one afternoon. I had begun moving to a new place but still had lots of things at the old place where he and I had apartments in the same complex. He was parked in my space, and parking was really bad there. I parked in my roommate's space and went up to get a few things. For some reason, I went to his apartment and knocked on the door. One of his roommates answered, but after I asked for him, he pushed the door closed to go and get him. This was unusual. He obviously didn't want me to see something. I knew at that moment that another girl was over there, and I turned and walked away with a sick feeling in my stomach. There is something to be said for women's intuition

CLOSURE CONVERSATION

— so don't ignore it. I went back to my apartment, got a few things and hurried out of the building. I had begun to cry because I knew that he was with someone else and I felt like such a fool. We had just had the conversation the night before that gave me hope, the "closure" conversation. From this experience I can offer you this advice: be sure to be honest about your expectations from this type of conversation. In most cases, if you *need* a "closure" conversation, you are not ready for closure.

I got in my car and drove off. About halfway in between my old place and the new one, I got angry and decided to go back and confront him. I don't know why, but all of a sudden, I was tired of feeling this way. I needed to know for sure that he was with someone. My return was perfect timing because, as I was driving up to the apartment, I saw him and he wasn't alone. He was with his cousin and the girl that he was involved with, we'll call her Girl #2, and they were walking toward his car that was parked in my parking space, getting ready to leave. I stopped my car right behind his so that he couldn't move and demanded to have a conversation right then.

As you could imagine, he was pissed off and wanted me to go home. This was not a good time for him to have such a conversation, but for me, there was no time like the present. I kept telling him that we needed to talk right then and that I was not going to move. He demanded that I move my car, but I would not. Instead, I got out of the car and began to confront him. I got up in his face in a rage, and he pushed me back. I pushed and grabbed him, and although I was met with his resistance, I would not stop. I remember him sort of holding me up against his car and yelling at Girl #2 to get back. I was so mad that I would have welcomed her to the brawl at the time, but looking back, I put myself in a really bad position. The bottom line was that he was with both of us because we allowed it. The physical match was just between the two of us, but not only could he have really hurt me but the others could have pitched in. Ladies, never put yourself in a dangerous position like this. It will not always turn out in your favor.

I didn't feel anything but anger and frustration, however, and I was determined to make him understand my feelings. He finally realized that I was not going to quit, got away from me, and headed toward his other car to drive off. I must have looked like a crazy fool to Girl #2, but I didn't care because I could not take the games any longer. I wanted off of this emotional roller coaster.

When we spoke of the incident much later, he told me that he told Girl #2 that I was crazy, and you can believe that my actions confirmed it for her. This brings me to the point. Men will often tell you that some other woman they "used to be involved with" is crazy to change the subject, and because we want so badly to hear about another woman's weakness to make us feel better about ourselves, we quickly accept his interpretation. Do not fall for that. Nine out of ten times, he's gaming you. There is the possibility that she may actually be crazy too, which means you need to be careful if there is another woman in his life who might actually hurt you; but trust me, if you have ever really been in a situation like this, you have been called the crazy one to the next chick he's trying to game.

CLOSURE CONVERSATION

As he left, I decided I wasn't going to let him get off that easily. I noticed that he dropped his car keys, and so I picked them up. I drove around to the security center and told them that someone had parked in my parking space and I wanted them to tow the car, which was common practice in the building. They quickly obliged, and I drove to my new home without my glasses, which I lost in the tussle, and with his keys. I was gratified for the moment, but after getting home, talking to one of my close girlfriends, and thinking about what I did, I was just tired and sad because my heart still ached for this man.

REAL TALK 5

Women tend to act like we don't care to know about the other woman, but the truth is that we do. We want to compare ourselves to the other one and come up with all of the reasons he should like us more than the other woman in his life. I've often heard women say that they didn't want to know about her, but the truth is that every woman wants to know about her competition if she has truly allowed a man into her heart. I mentioned that the other woman could well be crazy, and this advice is not to be taken lightly. You never know when a woman is at her breaking point over such a situation, and you never know what that means for your safety, especially if he's married.

CHAPTER SIX
Pregnant by Who?

I really wanted to know all of the details about what he was doing so that I could remain in my own driver's seat, but I knew that one day, because I had the kind of open communication I did with this man's roommates, I would find out something I didn't want to hear. One day, while having a conversation with his brother, who was also one of his roommates, the words "loose lips sink ships" came rolling off of his tongue after he discovered by the look on my face that he had told me something I never heard before. While I didn't think I had anything to worry about from the high school girlfriend back at home, his brother had just slipped and told me that my friend and his high school girlfriend had a baby girl together a couple of months earlier. I couldn't believe my ears. Appropriately, it was just before Mother's Day weekend. I cried as I drove home to see my mother for the holiday.

I couldn't believe that this man, whom I loved so much, was now a father. I was certainly not the one to end up pregnant at that time. I was in no way interested in having his baby or anyone else's, but I wasn't ready to let him go. Think about this: If you get pregnant and your family has to ask who you are pregnant by, you have no business being pregnant. I just needed to throw that out there. Now, where was I? I was not the only one who wasn't ready to let him go. I told you about Girl #2 and I mentioned that she would do anything for him. Though she had to be hurt, she seemed to go right on along with the program, or at least that was the way things appeared to me. His new baby's mother remained in Los Angeles in the beginning, but he would eventually bring her to northern California to try to work out a relationship between the two of them, for the baby's sake, he said.

I don't remember our exact conversation when we finally talked about his paternity. I do remember that he didn't open up too much to me, but he was of course curious as to how I found out. I would not tell him. He did tell me that he would be taking care of his daughter, which I expected from him, but he never mentioned whether he would be stopping any of his extra-curricular relationships or committing to anyone — which of course is what I was most curious about. He did neither. He knew that I would be mad at him for a while, but in the meantime, he continued as before with Girl #2. However, I was convinced that my relationship with him had to stop. The fact that he had a baby now, and that he didn't tell me about it, was too much. He obviously had no respect for me or our relationship, and so I finally realized that I needed to call it off and stick to that decision. I would not accept this treatment any longer. I was now trying to move on with my life once again, but I still could not cut off my feelings. Everything in me that knew better wanted so badly to move on, and I really tried, but my heart wouldn't let him go. I would ask God to please take the desire for this man away because he would not give me what I deserved: to be loved and respected, held in high regard even unto being treated like a queen. Ladies, remember that no matter how involved you are in a bad relationship situation, you still deserve to be loved and respected, and that even goes for high school girlfriend and Girl #2 in my situation.

Although, I know that my friend must have been changed by the birth of his daughter, his actions did not indicate he had really changed much at all. In fact, he continued to do the same things. I know that he was in a difficult position, but neither of the women he was involved with were willing to cut off the relationship, and so he didn't change. He didn't have to. We were still competing for his affection and his time, and he had a baby with another person who wasn't even in the equation as far as I had been concerned — this baby now put her in the equation for sure. I always knew that his high school girlfriend held a piece of his affection because of their history, but she wasn't real to me because she wasn't there. Girl #2 and I were more concerned with one another because we saw each other. I must tell you that I had no plans to go forward with him. I did not have any intentions on being in a relationship with a man who had a child with someone else, and if you have never thought about this and are fortunate enough not to have experienced this before, please decide now how you would deal with that situation should it arise. I strongly suggest that you think seriously about the scenario and how it could affect your life. Are you willing to accept a child by another woman, and if so, what does the scenario have to include in order for you to be happy in it?

When his daughter was about 1? years of age, he moved the baby and her mom to northern California to live with him. He told me that they were coming and that he was going to do the best thing for his daughter. I respected his decision and thought that I could handle that. I backed away and tried to move on with my life, which I was able to do, but only for a while. His plans were to stop all of his "extra relationships" so that he could try to work things out with his daughter's mother. I thought that he was doing the best thing and I decided to be his friend. I supported his decision. We did not talk as much, but every now and then, I would talk to him and find out how things were going.

He was busy helping his daughter's mom try to find a job. Things weren't working out like he thought, and so once we found her an apartment, she and the baby moved there but he continued to live with his roommates. You are not mistaken. I did say we found her an apartment. I helped him find her a place because I really was committed to the friendship, and in truth, things were cool between us as far as this friendship thing was going. To be honest, I guess I found a little comfort in the fact that I wasn't the only one who had lost him. I had always been okay with his daughter's mom being in his heart because of the history of their relationship, and as long as Girl #2 didn't win him, I could live with his choice not to be with me.

However, the next thing I knew, he was in a relationship with Girl #2, and this time, she had "the title." I was so hurt. I knew then that I needed to move on for sure. This time, I was seriously going to back off and try this friend thing once again but from a distance.

Girl, don't fool yourself into thinking that you can just be friends with someone you are in love with. Be realistic about your expectations. I mentioned earlier that I was willing to move to the side for his daughter's mom (and their baby girl), the one I knew nothing about, but there was that competition thing again with Girl #2. Although I knew my position regarding this man and friendship, I didn't know hers, and she was obviously willing to put up with a little less respect than I was when it came to a relationship with him. She totally messed up the game as far as I was concerned, and that's the problem. Too many of us get caught up in the game, but he's the one calling all of the shots.

At this point, I took things day by day. The situation was hard for me, but don't think that I did nothing but sit at home and wait for this guy to call me. I was not ready to give up on myself just yet. I was working a fulltime job, working on my Master's degree, and enjoying a very active social life. I didn't like going out with the girls all that much anymore because I was sick of meeting the same old guys with the same old baggage. But who was I to talk? Talk about baggage. I had not let go of my heartache either. I had made a decision though not to sit at home cut-off from the world. You better believe my friend was still out there doing his thing, and I decided to do the same. He and I had been through so many ups and downs and by this time we had a voluminous history. We were involved one minute and stopped all communication the next, but we still remained a small part of each other's lives no matter what. History. What is it really? We sometimes get so caught up with that word as if it is something to cherish, but if you've had a history of lies and deceit, pain and disrespect, is the history really worth holding on to?

School and work were working out great for me. I enjoyed school and looked forward to filling my time with something meaningful and effective. I was growing as a person and as a scholar, developing character and exploring a new world. Work put me in a position to take care of myself financially and to build a resume while enjoying life's little pleasures. No matter where I found myself emotionally, I was always around men who took an interest in me. It was flattering, but through it all, I wanted the one that I wanted. I entertained a few friendships with other guys, but in my heart, I was looking for someone to replace my "friend." I wanted to feel about someone else the way I felt about him. I'd meet different types of guys, and some of them had a genuine interest in me, but my heart knew the real thing was represented by this other guy, the one who had brought me so much grief.

Don't get me wrong. I appreciated the guys who came into my life during that time. They reminded me of how much I had to offer, how complete a package I was for that stage in my life. I'd meet guys at social gatherings, but I also managed to spark a few pretty solid friendships with guys I knew from work or school. I was looking for companionship, but I was unwilling to make a relationship happen with a friend just so that I could have someone around. I never wanted to hurt anyone's feelings, especially after being in that position myself. This reason alone meant that I couldn't ever be a "player." Been there, done that, and so how could I do the same thing to someone else?

I continued passing time with friends, hanging out and talking out my feelings regarding the last situation, but I never led anyone on. I was really trying to be honest about my position, and despite this fact, a few of my male friends, quite aware of how I was hurt in my previous relationship, still came to care for me in a way that invited more than just a regular friendship. They truly were jewels, but they were men and so would have been willing to take whatever I was willing to give, just in case I wanted to have a "friends with benefits" type relationship. Some men's hearts are actually in the right place, but no man needs all that a woman does to get something going, especially something physical. If you are in a situation like this, one in which other men are looking to comfort you in ways that exceed mere friendship, know what you are doing. It's easy to get caught up if you are not careful.

Just as things seemed to be working out for me, I ran into my "old friend." You can never get far enough away when you live in close proximity to an old situation. We were both pretty excited to see each other, and he was also glad to report that he was sending his daughter's mom back home because the relationship wasn't working out. He was a little sad though that he would not get to see his daughter as often, which was no surprise to me. He didn't know that I had heard about his more solid relationship with Girl #2, but of course I couldn't resist asking about her, since we were just "friends" anyway. I don't remember my exact words, but I wanted to know how it happened that he became re-involved with Girl #2. I didn't get an answer, not one worth remembering anyway. As you could guess, he didn't want to talk about that.

My feelings for him were as strong as ever but I was going to stay in the driver's seat this time. I remained calm and friendly as we talked about what was going on in his life, but not too friendly. I needed to be sure I did not fall back into the same trap. After a few weeks, we were back on pretty regular speaking terms. He never asked me about any other guys, friendships or relationships that I was forming, and because there was no one significant, there was no need to bring it up. I was playing my "friend" cards right, and we even made plans to hang out at some point in the future.

The friendship program was coasting right along, until one day I got the news that he had broken his leg playing basketball. My heart melted. The tough exterior I was trying to build up with him was broken into pieces. Here we were getting our friendship together, and I wanted to run to his rescue because I knew that he was "out of the game." This accident was going to take a toll on him, and I felt so bad for him. I didn't need to feel bad though, because he had a "girlfriend," and she was of course at his beck and call. There was nothing left for me to do. It really was a good thing that this Girl # 2 was in the picture, but I wanted to be there for him so badly it hurt.

All I could think about was the fact that I wanted him to know that I was there for him, and if he needed anything he could call on me. "STUPID." I told myself this all the time. I knew that it was stupid to want to comfort him, but my heart was determined to somehow get the message to him that I could be there for him. I really challenged myself over those previous months not to call him, but there was nothing other than willpower stopping me — his number hadn't changed. That willpower was now completely gone out of the door. I had to make that call, and I did. In short, I lost a few points.

Ladies, ladies, ladies. An emotional event like that can break us down. Don't think of such things as emotional though. This man's accident was a physical life lesson for him. He needed to slow down, and someone with a certain HIGHER POWER was emphatically making the point. I knew that at the time, but I couldn't stay angry enough to hold my position. Darn. Just as I was making huge strides toward my emancipation, I faltered. A day or so after I made that call, I was completely disappointed with myself.

REAL TALK 6

Sometimes we come to a point where it would really benefit us if we could stand up for ourselves, and in doing so, stand up for what is right, making these boys step up and become responsible men, but we don't. We'd rather try to grab him while the other girl is out of the picture, or so we think.

Remember, thinking that we can be friends with him when he has other things going on and we're still in love with him is to enter really dangerous territory. There are so many other guys out there to be friends with, some who actually respect you and will support you. Investigate what it is like to really be friends with a member of the opposite sex. Learn a man's heart, how he thinks, and whether you'd ever really be able to make it with the one you think you love. Some women have never been treated with love and respect by any man, which is the reason these women expect so little from all men. Be real about your expectations when you use the word "friend." Be honest and true to yourself. Remember that little voice I mentioned previously: most of the time, that voice is warning us, but we don't want to hear the truth and so we tune it out. Listen to the voice of God in you — most of the time it's right.

CHAPTER SEVEN
Making it Through

I was going through a host of other things in my life during the time that all of this drama was taking place, and I knew that this relationship had taken so much out of me that I had to stop it. I decided to figure out why I wanted this man so badly, hoping that maybe this newfound understanding would help me to resolve my feelings for this guy. I tried to rationalize my behavior, but as we all know, love is not rational. I had stopped talking to my close girlfriends about him long ago because even I had gotten sick of hearing the stories. I needed a confidant, someone with some insight beyond what I had been able to discover up to that point, and I found someone, a counselor. You may think that I was a little crazy by now, and I thought so too at the time, but I had to be sure.

I was on a quest to discover who I was. I wanted to know how my mind would allow my heart to get so caught up. My family life and upbringing kept coming up in my heart, and so I had to find out what, if anything, my upbringing had to do with my current choices. I could not understand how I had gotten to the point of loving someone who could not love me the way I deserved to be loved. Throughout all of the terrible things that I had put up with from this man, I never lost sight of the fact that I deserved to be truly loved and respected but didn't know how to get that from him. As a matter of fact, I had never really known that kind of love and respect in my relationship with him. This was my true struggle. After all, I was an ideal candidate, so why was I allowing him to take so much of my heart and play with it like it was a cheap toy. The reason that kept coming to mind even then was love, and that was not the answer that I wanted hear.

The counselor reaffirmed for me all that I knew I was. He also helped me to realize that I had given a lot of control to my friend and that he may not have been as bad a guy as he seemed to be to me. Because I apparently saw something positive in him, not just the bad things, this made me feel better about my decision to involve myself with him at all. We sometimes forget amidst our own drama that other people also have things that they are going through. I felt like my upbringing was having an impact on my love and relationship decisions, but I failed to consider what impact my friend's upbringing was having on his. The counselor, who was also a Black male, agreed that my friend obviously saw something in me from the stories I had shared with him. Although this was my opinion, it was encouraging to hear it from someone else who had no interest one way or the other. I know this sounds strange, but I felt better knowing that I wasn't in love with someone who was a blatant loser from another person's perspective. Beware, however: sometimes the guys you fall for are losers.

MAKING IT THROUGH

I told my counselor the raw and unvarnished truth about my friend and me. I had imagined the worst case scenario, and it didn't sting as much when the truth mirrored my impression. The counselor simply listened and responded without ripping me to shreds for being so stupid in love. I must admit that, sometimes, when I have listened to many of my friend's dramas with their guys, I wish I could be as eloquent as he was when he responded to my tales of woe. I have given many people support and advice and spread lots of truth on this very difficult topic, and I know that some of it has hurt — the truth sometimes does. In many cases, I had to share a dose of reality, or what I refer to as "Real Talk," but it was the same talk that I was saying to myself over and over again. In fact, this straight talk is what the counselor provided for me, but in many instances he was only repeating what I had heard that little voice saying in my head all along.

The time had come for both my friend and I to graduate from college. This would be the second time for me and my friend would earn his degree in social work. His leg had healed, and so things had gotten back to normal for the most part. He and I were now spending more time together, and our friendship was moving in a positive direction. We actually became very good friends over the last semester before graduating, and things between him and Girl #2 were what they were. I tried to stop asking questions that I didn't want to know the answer to. I had decided that I was not going to worry about his relationship with her and that I was going to enjoy our friendship without trying to pursue anything more. I was exceptionally proud of him on graduation day. He had come from a background of tragedy, difficulties, and hard times, but he made it through, despite the long odds.

His story had made such an impression on me that I nominated him the "Most Inspirational" graduating senior. Of course, the fact that I was in love with him had something to do with why I put so much into the nomination letter, but I truly believed in my heart that he was worthy of the honor. The fact that he had overcome so much was directly related to what I saw in him and why I thought so much of him.

My friend grew up in Watts in South Central Los Angeles, an area plagued by drugs and gangs, violence and poverty. My friend, like many living in urban areas across America, grew up witnessing drive-by shootings, went to dilapidated schools and was the product of a faltering educational system. He also witnessed alcohol abuse, unemployment, homelessness, and the list goes on. What does it take to make it out of such a situation if one grows up in an area where there isn't much promise of a good life, or even of any life beyond the age of 20? An even greater issue at hand for my friend and others in such urban areas was growing up in a single parent household headed by a female, which meant a lack of male role models, and too often, of any positive images of Black males at all.

My friend was dealt a difficult hand from the start, beginning with the loss of his mother to domestic violence when he was six years old. He was the oldest of three brothers, one two years younger and the other not even a year old. He recalled the day for me that his mother sent him along with his brothers around the corner to their aunt's apartment, which was in the same housing complex, better known as "the projects." The last thing she said to him was "take care of your brothers" as she hugged them and sent them on their way. He has a few very fond memories of his mother prior to her death, but he had no idea of the obstacles that were yet to come from simply having no mother of his own.

My friend ended up living with several family members as a child. Although each of his brothers ended up going to a different aunt, my friend moved from relative to relative, having to change schools and make new friends each time. Living by yet another person's house rules and fitting into their immediate family structure was difficult to adjust to.

My friend remembers overhearing the conversations between his family members after his mother's death regarding how to proceed as far as her children were concerned. With the boys being so young, it was a lot for the other family members to take on when many of them had children of their own and a lack of resources to take care of them. My friend never really opened up about his emotions surrounding his childhood, but this particular memory struck a nerve with him. He remembered that the adults were willing to take his brothers because they were younger, but he told me, "No one wanted me." Although it seems unlikely that his family would have actually said that, he had been carrying this on his heart all of this time. My heart broke as he told me his feelings. I grew up with both of my parents for the most part, and therefore I could hardly imagine how difficult it must have been for him. He said that he walked on eggshells in the houses of his relatives because he was grateful that someone cared enough to eventually take him in.

He started out living with his great grandma and then his godmother. Eventually, however, his mother's aunt retrieved him because she felt like he was too far from his extended family. Over the years, he ended up living with his mom's cousin, then his aunt, and eventually with another aunt with whom he found a little stability. Each time he moved, he had to change schools and adjust to a new environment, which had much to do with how he'd become so social and friendly. His relatives also lived in and around the projects, and so the environment did not improve for him. He began hanging out with the wrong crowd, joined gangs, robbed and stole, smoked and drank because these were the things going on in the neighborhood. He was out there alone, with no real guidance, hustling and feeling obligated to assist his aunt with things like bringing in money and taking care of her younger children. He was around 11 years old at the time. His aunt ended up falling on difficult times after the death of her husband, however, and lost her own children to the foster care system — and my friend was off to yet another family member.

Before this next transition, my friend had been witness to more death than any person should see much less a pre-teenage child. He even had a few close brushes with death himself, which is not all that uncommon for youth in poor urban areas. He finally ended up in a stable living environment where he had a positive and influential male role model, and that fact began to make a difference for him. He was living with another one of his mother's cousins, and although she had a few of her own personal issues, she was educated, had a husband who was gainfully employed, and did not live in the projects. This was the first time he ever experienced things as simple as salads with dinner and eating out at even the most modest places. These are such small events, and most of us take these things for granted.

Up to this point in his life, every male that my friend encountered had been involved with gangs and sold drugs, used or abused drugs and/or alcohol, didn't take care of their children, and had several women at a time. This had an impact on how he saw himself in relationships, and it also shaped how he saw women and men in general. He did not know his biological father, and with his mother being deceased, no one seemed to have any answers for him that were positive. However, not everything that he experienced in the "hood" was negative because he was exposed to entrepreneurship, hustling to make something of himself when opportunities weren't rampant, as well as things like developing family-type relationships beyond his blood relatives.

After this move, my friend also found more time to spend with his first love, basketball, which was a great skill he developed while hanging out in the neighborhood. For the first time, he was doing well in school, and basketball introduced him to more positive male role models in the form of coaches, who had a major impact on his future. His cousin's husband became his father figure, but my friend only stayed in that living situation for a couple of years because his cousin threatened to stop him from playing basketball. He packed up a few things in his backpack one day on the way to school and never went back. He ended up living with his great aunt, the one who had gone to pick him up from his godmother's several years before. She was taking care of many of the kids in his family who were left to raise themselves, and so he was just another head to count and mouth to feed in this new situation. After about a year and a half there, basketball had earned my friend a scholarship to an all-boys boarding high school in Virginia, which was a long way from the hood. Thanks to one of his coaches and God, a way was made for him to pursue real success. My friend earned a basketball scholarship to San Jose State University, which is where we met, and now he was graduating from college with a Bachelor's degree.

He was selected to be the Master of Ceremony at our graduation, and we were both really excited about this achievement. Many of the people we started college with had not been fortunate enough to make it to that point. I had been blessed to win the position as Speaker, and I wanted to present my class and all of our guests with a wonderful uplifting message of encouragement. I graduated with a 3.97GPA from my Master's program, and the audience recognized my accomplishment with applause.

I'll never forget the incredible sense of both admiration and joy I felt though when the Chairperson of the Graduation Committee read a few of my exact words from the letter I had poured out in support of my friend's nomination to be the "Most Inspirational Student," which he was awarded at this ceremony. The letter went something like this:

It is with extreme pleasure that I tender this nomination on behalf of _____. _____, who is an extremely optimistic and hardworking young man. He has an outgoing personality and is comfortable initiating and implementing new ideas and plans of action. He is a member of a fraternity and has taken an active leadership role, serving as both Corresponding Secretary and Vice President of his undergraduate chapter. He was a member of the basketball team, where he displayed his skills as both a leader and a team player. He is currently a fulltime student, holds two part-time jobs, and has a beautiful two year-old baby girl.

I went on to include a little bit of his story, which contributed greatly to why he was selected.

This young man has beaten the odds. He grew up in South Central Los Angeles in an environment full of hardships and hopelessness. He lost his mother to domestic violence at an early age and has never known his biological father. Despite such tragedies, he has remained positive and grateful for the support that he has gotten from his family. He has demonstrated his appreciation by giving back to his family and his community in abundance.

_____ is very passionate about helping those who are less fortunate, and he is dedicated to improving the quality of life for others. He has worked hard to maintain his grade point average and has a very active social life as well. He is very friendly and giving, and he is definitely an inspiration to his peers.

I'm not sure that this young man has ever been acknowledged for his dedication and perseverance, but I don't know anyone who is more deserving of this award. I nominate _____ because he is not the typical recipient of awards or honors like this, but his triumph should certainly be recognized. We need the type of example this person represents, the type of example that can be looked at as living proof in our community.

It is without further reservation that I nominate _____.

By now, I had further developed who I was, and I had also developed my definition of a man. With the exception of the foul things he had done to me and the other young ladies over the course of the past few years, my friend really was a good person. He exemplified many qualities that were important to me as a woman who was not privileged myself, and I meant every word of the letter, which elucidated some of what I saw in this man that attracted me to him so strongly in the first place.

I suggest that, when choosing the person to share the rest of your life with, you try writing a nomination letter of this sort to your family or to the world, a letter outlining why they too should believe in your choice. You should have things to say about this man that are closely aligned with your views on life, your values, your philosophy. Be really honest about these things, however, because if you can't be honest with yourself, then who can you be honest with? If you can't find enough positive things to include in the letter, perhaps you haven't really found the one yet. I thought I did, but obviously, I also had many bad things to say about him, as reflected in my conversations with my counselor. However, just outlining his positive attributes helped me to further define my idea of a man, and for that I am grateful to the exercise.

This day was full of hope, but wouldn't you know it, amidst those cheerful memories, one of my friend's relatives invited Girl #2 to dinner with them to celebrate. Boy, what could I say — I couldn't win for losing.

REAL TALK 7

I know you want to know how I could tell you in one breath how much pain this man caused me and in the same breath tell you how great a person he was. My relationship with him was really sort of like that. Great one minute, horrible the next, but I obviously thought the good outweighed the bad. I believed in his character, but you have to ask yourself the same questions I had to ask myself: Is he really of good character or do you want someone so badly that you are looking through rose-colored glasses to see what you want to see? Did his background and upbringing really spell potential or did it point to disaster? How much should I let his upbringing influence my decision because, after all, my heart is being broken time and time again and I am important here? You must also remember that just because someone deserves better or even deserves praise doesn't mean that you have to be the one to give it to him. You also have to ask yourself, "Girl, do you really want to spend the rest of your life with him or are you trying to win the competition with the other woman?"

MAKING IT THROUGH

*If he don't want you then he ain't for you
but who can be against you when God is for you?
Remember that rejection is God's gift of protection
so don't feel so bad about it.*
—N. Crawford

Part Two
the Fight

CHAPTER EIGHT
Prize or Not?

Things had begun to go in a whole new direction. My friend and I were spending a lot more time together, and I was trying my best not to ask too many questions and go along with the program. I wanted to know where our relationship was going, but I did my best to hold off on pushing things and enjoy the time for what it was. We were planning to get down to San Diego for a few days after graduation, but as it turned out, we headed to Los Angeles instead, where he would be visiting family and I would be visiting some friends. We ended up stopping by my family reunion along the way and hung out with several of my relatives. They were pleased with him, and I was excited that he had actually gotten the chance to meet more of them, including my mother. I always felt like once someone had the opportunity to meet my family, they'd understand me better, and not to mention, my folks have always been lots of fun. It meant a lot to me that he was open to it. Once we were in LA, he also introduced me to several of his family members at a celebration that they were having in honor of his graduation. As it turned out, this trip was more meaningful than I had expected.

We returned home to northern California, and things were working out pretty well for us. We started having those life conversations that I longed for, the ones that provided an outlook on the possibility of us having a future together, including a committed relationship. We were now talking about the type of woman he really saw himself with versus what he had been settling for during college. Interestingly enough, the fact that he had a daughter and wanted her to be of substance and quality when she grew up had begun to affect his decision making — thank goodness. I was impressed that he paid attention to the things that I thought were important, wanting them for his own daughter. I knew for certain that I had a chance over the other women that he had involved himself with because I was the woman he was describing when he talked about who his daughter would become. I was the influence that she needed, and I thought I'd be willing to play the part.

We had now known each other for three years, and good and bad things had happened, but now I was nearly in heaven. We were both working at the county's juvenile hall, and so we spent even more time together. Sometimes we would ride together to and from work, and our conversations during these rides became more and more intense, focusing on the future. What I wanted most from him was a commitment — I wanted the title. I wanted to be his "girlfriend" and have all of the rights that came along with the designation. I wanted to drop by his house without calling first. I wanted to have a guaranteed date. I wanted someone to share my time with even if I wasn't doing much. But most of all, I wanted him to give me something that I deserved: love and respect. I wanted to be the sole object of his affection as he had so long been the object of mine.

Although things were going great, there was still that question in the back of my mind. What was going on with Girl #2? One thing that I had learned several years earlier was that a man will make time for what he wants to do, including spending time with other women, no matter how much of his time you think you take up. I just shake my head when I hear women explain that their men don't have time to cheat because he's always with them. I remember thinking that very thought in the beginning, and I remember learning very quickly that a man will make a way to get what he wants. What must she be thinking now that he had been spending so much time with me? Does she know? One thing I thought for sure was that she knew he wasn't with her. Keep in mind though that you never really know how a man explains his time or justifies his whereabouts to his girlfriend or even his wife. I got around to asking my friend about Girl #2, but as I expected, he didn't provide me with much insight. Mostly I kept quiet and carried on with life as usual. It was almost freaky. I had gotten used to being in such a position of defeat with him that I never saw myself being this close to victory.

I remember feeling at times like a sixth man on the bench. I played basketball when I was younger and related my experience with my friend to sitting on the sideline, waiting to go in as I wondered if the coach would recognize my progress and really good attitude in practice that week — only to have him say he was going to call me in with a couple of minutes left on the clock and yet I still sat there. With only a few minutes left in the game, I had given up, and I found it hard to hide my disappointment. I didn't want to spend our time together arguing or asking questions that I really didn't want to know the answer to anyway, and so I just "sucked it up" and sat in my spot on the bench.

I let Girl #2 escape farther and farther from my mind when my friend and I were together, but I kept my feelers out otherwise. I wanted to know if anyone had seen her around, or more importantly, if anyone had seen them together. While I was busy wondering about such trivial things, there were a few other things that I didn't think of as so important but that kept coming up nevertheless.

I arrived home from work one day, and I was in a good mood because I knew that I could expect my friend to be there later on that evening. He was at my apartment when I left for work, and I knew that he would be returning. When he returned though, he had something on his mind. While I was gone, he had done something that I'm pretty sure he had never done with me before. He read my journal, and there was something in there that he did not want to see. Around that time, I had written several passages in the journal about how much pain he was putting me through, but wouldn't you know it, he'd skip over all of that and read the passage about a friend of mine who managed to get some of my time while the man in my living room and I were at odds. There was nothing bad about this in "real life," but he was so angry at me that he almost walked away. There was really nothing juicy in the journal, but he was so upset with me because he knew the guy I mentioned and I had never bothered to tell him about my relationship with this person.

Listen, ladies. Some things are worth mentioning and others are not, and each of us must judge for ourselves and be smart about it. I had not mentioned this other guy to my friend because ours was nothing more than a platonic relationship. Sure I knew that he had feelings for me that exceeded friendship, but there was no reason for me to get my old friend worked up any further by telling him about that. To be honest, I wasn't sure where things were even going with my old friend or how long it would last, but I wasn't going to do anything to ruin that. My decision was that this other relationship was better left secret.

Because they knew each other, which was very difficult to avoid in the college world, my platonic friend had actually gone to my old friend during our bad times to remind him of what a good catch I was. I never asked him to do this, but I think he really felt bad for me. I must admit that I was flattered that my friend was upset. Don't get me wrong. The man sitting in my living room had completely caught me off guard, but I wasn't even upset with him for reading my journal, which is a violation to say the least. I actually felt excited because he was so angry with me because, for the first time, he was hurt and showed a little emotion for something that had to do with me. I now knew that I was getting somewhere — he cared. It's so strange that women are always looking for the little clues that a man cares, but the question becomes, "What do we do with that?" Sometimes they care simply because it is difficult not to have some attachment to someone who cares for you so much, but what does that really mean? Caring for you doesn't necessarily stop them from caring for someone else or mistreating you. As long as we know, however, that caring is never expressed with violence, we're good — or so it seems.

I whispered to my roommate, who was witnessing this whole exchange, that he was mad at me and why, and she and I both giggled. I then composed myself and turned to face my friend. I couldn't let him know that I thought this was funny while he was angry with me. Men can be so sensitive. My little scenario was hardly revenge, however. In fact, it didn't even compare.

It was not long before we were past this minor snafu and back on happy trails. Things were really good, in fact, especially the day that a portion of the song Sweet Lady by Tyrese was written in a letter to me and my "old friend" finally declared himself my "new boyfriend." FINALLY, I HAD WON. But what exactly did I win? Sometimes we get so caught up in the fight that we forget what we are fighting for or whether there is actually a PRIZE to win. It took three years and four months, but now I would have the commitment that I longed for with the man I wanted. Time would tell another tale.

The year was winding down, and my boyfriend and I were making plans for our future. It felt so good to finally call him "my boyfriend," and I know you know just what I mean. However, although I knew that he was planning on moving back home to Los Angeles so that he could be a part of his daughter's life, which was noble, I was in no way going to invite myself along. We began having conversations about my relocating with him, and I had only one reservation. We would first have to make our new relationship work in the same city where all of the drama had taken place before I was comfortable that we could move away and have a trusting and committed relationship. He didn't reject the idea, and after some planning and preparation, some testing to see if the relationship would hold in this town, we moved to Los Angeles to start our new life together.

Prior to leaving northern California though, we started to work on and think about business ventures that we would pursue in our new home. Not only were we beginning our lives together, but we were both new college graduates and had high hopes of putting our degrees to work. He had lined up a job, and we had a place to live waiting. We were saving money and continued to prepare things so that we'd have a smooth transition. Although I had looked for work consistently, I found nothing worthy of my time or talent, nor anything that even compared with the job that I had at the time, counseling at juvenile hall. My boyfriend encouraged me to take all of the time I needed until something good enough came along. I was a little anxious about that, but I was actually looking for an opportunity to utilize my Master's degree and I knew that this would be no easy task. I also had no interest in going back to the juvenile justice system. I felt like I was making an important contribution there, but my interests were changing and I really wanted to pursue goals that were more in line with my educational background. I always felt that my boyfriend would spend a lifetime working in this field because he had that kind of heart. It's very important to get to know your partner, including where they come from, so that you might understand where they are headed. You can never know everything, but the fewer surprises, the better.

While at home, I started developing an idea that I had long ago to start a business that would serve young women. My boyfriend and I continued to work on that project together, but we were also researching other things. We decided that we would focus more energy on this project while I was still at home and looking for work. I was now in a great place in my relationship, but I was in a personal place I had not been. I did not have a job, and although we planned for this, I couldn't help feeling like I needed to carry my own weight. I started considering jobs that I was overqualified for because I needed to have something. My boyfriend would come home from work every day renewed and reenergized, reiterating that I had nothing to worry about because I would find the job that I was looking for.

We spent our free time getting to know the city and visiting the different places that he knew as a child. I loved getting to know more and more about his life and his family. I honestly believe that it pays to do this together, to spend time getting to know each other's past. Things from the past, yours and his, will resurface. It's human nature. Sometimes, we place undue pressure on ourselves though. I needed a job because I didn't want a man to have to take care of me. I wanted my independence, which is a sign of the times, but I also wanted to be

PRIZE OR NOT?

in a relationship with a man. In short, there were a few things that I needed to learn. I didn't know it at the time, but God was setting me up to become more humble by having to rely for the first time on a man other than my father, which I believe strengthened our relationship.

Three months after moving away, my boyfriend interviewed with a nonprofit organization. He had come to the conclusion that this was the perfect job for me. He told them that he wasn't interested in the position, but that he had the perfect person for them. He told them about me. I went in a few days later for an interview and was hired on the spot. I'd found a job that met my expectations — *or rather he'd found the job* — a job with an organization that recognized my qualifications and compensated me nicely. My interview was on a Friday and I started on the following Monday.

Previously, I mentioned that my boyfriend had planned *since his daughter's return* to go back home to Los Angeles upon graduating from college. He had no plans to be with his daughter's mom, but she must have had other ideas. I'll never forget the message he played for me prior to moving to LA. His high school girlfriend and the mother of his child confessed to him in anger that he would never see his daughter again. We had no idea at the time what he was in for, but we would soon find out.

Girl #2 was completely out of the picture, but high school girlfriend had reemerged with a vengeance. She could not believe that he would bring someone back with him to her territory and that he expected to build a relationship with their daughter to include another woman. Things were about to get ugly. You see, I was the competition she didn't know about. She was prepared for Girl #2, but she wasn't ready for all that I was. I never wanted to have problems with her, and I didn't expect to because my boyfriend and I were in a different place altogether. I knew that I was going to have to respect her because she was the mother of his child, but I would never end up getting around to that.

REAL TALK 8

Girl, pick and choose your battles wisely. Not everyone is worth the fight. In order to be successful in a relationship with someone else, you'll win some and you'll lose some — so accept that. **Compromise is key.** Remember, I told you to get to know your competition because you could be in a race you can't win. Keep in mind that not every man is boyfriend material, and not every boyfriend is a prize.

CHAPTER NINE
Baby Momma Drama

This has been an extremely difficult chapter for me to write, primarily because an innocent child was involved. Perhaps in writing it though, a light may come on for someone in a similar situation and they might realize their own impact in ways that they never have before. At times, all that I witnessed for the sake of a man trying to do the right thing, the moral thing for his child, was almost surreal. As God is my witness, this is the truth. I have started to write about this several times now, but I wasn't ready to come to terms with it. I guess now I'm ready.

Our trip to Los Angeles in preparation for our move should have been a sign of things to come. My boyfriend had made plans to see his daughter while he was visiting home because it had been several months since he'd last seen her. From the time of the official breakup and return to Los Angeles, communication with his high school girlfriend hadn't been so cordial. He'd made calls to arrange time with his daughter, but whether or not he'd actually get to spend any time with their daughter was still up in the air. Things weren't looking too hopeful from the outset and only went downhill from there.

One night during our stay, we were at his relative's home. This particular family member had a little history with his daughter's mom, as most of his relatives did, and she had a few choice words for her prior to leaving for work. I'll never forget, in the middle of a very heated and angry conversation, his family member said to his daughter's mom, screaming at the top of her lungs, "You are mad because you had the baby to keep the man and now you have the baby and still don't have the man." It sounded to me like they were referring to her as a human female version of a man's best friend. I was blown away and thought to myself, "Well, I guess she told her. Wow!"

His daughter's mom decided that this conversation wasn't over, and a couple of hours later, she dropped by the house unannounced. My boyfriend and I were relaxing in the back bedroom, watching television after the real-life drama had died down, but the real drama was about to begin. Although she'd come over to "talk" with the lady she had spoken with a little earlier, who had gone to work by now, the discovery that I was there, another woman who was obviously with her daughter's father, shifted her focus and she started to attack. She swung and slapped me on the side of my face, catching me off guard, I must admit, at which time, my boyfriend jumped between us and began forcing her toward the door. I reacted in an instant, jumping toward her to retaliate; but shortly thereafter, the strangest thing happened. I really wasn't all that angry and realized that I was in a very unique position. I had never been the one on that side of the coin with him, and I remember looking at her with such pity. I felt sorry for her.

I thought this time I should remain calm while I watched her make a complete fool out of herself. I didn't want my boyfriend to have two irrational women on his hands. Her friend was in the car with their child, and after putting her out of the house and onto the front porch, she left with the knowledge that her daughter's father was in his home with another woman yet she was exactly what his family member had said earlier: with baby and still *without* the man. I'm sure she felt good about getting a lick in on me, but after she left, my boyfriend and I relaxed in the Jacuzzi and thought about how we would spend the rest of our time in LA. Of course, I was heated at the time that this was going on; but simultaneously, I wasn't even worried about it. I was irritated that she did not even know about me and yet she directed all of her anger toward me, but I also assumed that she didn't care because she needed to let her pain out. I'd been there, which was the strangest realization. He was the one who decided not to see her anymore, but women often find it easier to take our pain and frustration out on the other woman. It's easier than dealing with the reality that the man that you love doesn't love you anymore, especially when you lost your chance to really hold on to him.

A few short months later, we made our move to Los Angeles; but after several months, my boyfriend was still unable to see his baby, who was going to be three years old soon and he really wanted to be in her life. He tried to reason with her mom, but she was too angry with him to even think about letting him see their child. She wouldn't even entertain a decent conversation. He now lived in LA with me and there was no way that she was going to let him see "her" baby. I must explain that I had no intention of trying to interfere in his relationship with his daughter, and I was not yet interested in being a mom myself. I'd had time to adjust to the idea that he had a child, but now, it was real. The baby was there, and as a woman, I was firm in my commitment that I would not step on the baby's mother's toes because one day I too might be a mother.

To be honest, this woman helped me out a lot by keeping their daughter away. He would have taken their child everyday had she asked, and I wasn't ready for that much time with a child. I hadn't been around young children very much, and so I didn't know how well I would do. Our relationship was still in its developmental stage, and I wanted us to spend as much time as possible getting to know each other. She also used his daughter against him, which made him despise her, and she drove us that much closer together. If she wanted him back, she was really messing up. I kicked back and watched this drama unfold, supporting him during his feelings of sadness at the absence of his baby girl. Although I understood the baby momma's pain, I never understood how she could put her daughter in the middle of this struggle, knowing the damage that it would cause their child. All in all, I never got to tell her thanks, however.

If you are keeping your child from seeing the father because he has moved on with his life, especially if he has found someone else yet you still have feelings for him, you are not making the situation better. He will never forgive you for that in the long run. You are making things worse for yourself and your child while leaving him no option but to find support in other arms. Think about it.

After much consideration, my boyfriend decided that he was going to take her to court. Although they had agreed never to involve the courts a few years earlier, he felt that this was the only thing that he could do to see his daughter. He drafted the Order to Show Cause asking the courts to help him get time with his child. It usually takes months to get a court date, and this instance was no exception. When we finally made it to court, she told the judge that their daughter was scared of her father and that he might have a violent flashback because his mother was killed in a domestic dispute (amongst a host of other untruths). Nevertheless, the judge decided to give him joint physical and legal custody of their daughter, requiring them to work with a court mediator to arrange a schedule. The child's mother tried to fight the decision, but the courts didn't allow it. This day in court was pretty fair to both parties, but it was only the beginning.

His first day of visitation came a few weeks later, and he gladly picked his daughter up from daycare. About an hour later, his daughter's mom and her mother showed up at our apartment building claiming that he had kidnapped their daughter and called the police. She told them that it wasn't even his daughter and that he had taken her, making a huge commotion. After showing the paperwork to the officer, they dismissed her and her mom, making them leave the building. I thought to myself, "What is the real problem here?" I knew, however, that the problem was me. As much of the unnecessary drama unfolded, which my being there obviously fueled, I wasn't going to leave my man so that she would be happy. My happiness counted here, and although I cared about his daughter's happiness, his ex had convinced herself that I was the problem. I'm sure she knew when she went to bed alone at night that the real problem was her.

Now the telephone calls started: Your daughter needs this. I need you to do that. She had gotten completely unreasonable now. Phone calls supposedly from Girl #2 started mysteriously once the baby's mother realized that I might answer the phone — high school girlfriend was up to high school games. The situation was getting so bad that his father tried to offer support to their situation by being an unbiased third party along with the ex's mom, for the child's sake. I was beginning to get a little tired of the games now, because my boyfriend was trying to do everything for his daughter and the child's mother had reneged on every arrangement they had made this far. I was not involved most of the time, but I had grown tired of seeing him trust that she was going to do her part only to be met with constant disappointment. He eventually got fed up and said enough is enough. I had reached my end point long before, but I did my best to swallow my pride because this wasn't about me — it was about his daughter. It takes a lot for this man to get fed up, but by now he was tired of his little girl being used as a pawn in this rotten power struggle against him. He didn't want her to suffer and was losing more and more respect for his daughter's mom. Now she had legitimately earned the title of a "baby momma."

For those who are not aware of the fact, "baby momma" is not a positive term. It is normally used to refer to someone who causes unnecessary drama for their children and the father(s) once their relationship goes bad, if there ever was one. She will not be the wife, and she's probably not a good mom because she uses her child as a pawn, thinking first of her own anger even before her children's happiness. Don't take this definition as one that degrades single mothers because that is not the point at all. I commend women who are doing the best they can to provide for and raise their children on their own. Those of you who fit this definition are not a "baby momma," but those of you who take advantage of this privilege of having children, I can only hope that you will one day "get it." There are "baby daddies" out there too, men who don't fight in court to be a part of their children's lives and who disappear. Although I think that a child is always worth the fight, however, I understand why some men choose not to be involved at all when the struggle is with a baby momma.

By now, court ordered time meant nothing more to his baby momma than the arrangements they had made before. She discovered that she could do what she wanted because the burden of proof was on him. He was the one who wanted to see their daughter, the petitioner in court. He was supposed to be added to her school emergency card, for example, but this never happened; and she would keep their daughter out of school on the day that he was supposed to pick her up so that he would miss his scheduled time. She never allowed his daughter to call him. It amazed me that there seemed to be absolutely nothing he could do about it. The courts did nothing. When it seemed that things were going somewhat smoothly for a while, we knew that something was up. In fact, she found another way to try to get him back. She went to child support court, which is separate from court for custody in California, and told them that he had never given her a dime of support for their daughter.

We were stunned. For the longest time, he never thought that he would have to go back and gather all of his receipts that he managed to keep here and there throughout his later college years. Now for the test. We were pulling receipts out of shoeboxes and notebooks and all sorts of places. Before we moved to Los Angeles, we talked about having to prove child support payments. Much to his dismay, he never thought that she would say he had not given her any financial support for their child. He gave both himself and her a little too much credit, if you ask me. In fact, the amount of confidence some men have in themselves when it comes to women might surprise you. "Hell hath no fury like a woman scorned," as Shakespeare said, and that was a tough life lesson he was about to learn.

Although he wasn't really worried about proving payments, I had held on to a couple of receipts for money orders that I had actually gotten for him. Once we decided that we were moving together, we started saving money together and he'd asked me to pick up money orders for him a few times to send to his daughter's mom with money that he'd given me to put up in savings. I'd happily oblige. Later on, once we were living in LA and both working, I would get cashier's checks directly from the bank to pay her from our joint account once a month.

She told the courts that this man had never given her a dime even though she had no steady job and was not on public assistance the first couple of years of their daughter's life. She had even written a letter to the District Attorney, which they had on file, telling them that she was living with him at one point and that he was taking care of their child. The District Attorney acted on her behalf, and the burden of proof was once again on him. Knowing that he had been taking care of his daughter, he wasn't worried at all. He'd gathered all of his receipts, placed them all in a folder, and began this process with the child support courts. Because he was at work in the day time, he had to try and get information while he was there. He dialed one telephone number after another and was sent around in circles daily. He'd finally made his way down to the District Attorney's office with receipts in hand only to discover that he needed to go to the child support court office on the other side of town because they didn't handle those matters there. Child Support Court, Court for Custody, and the District Attorney's office were located in three completely different places, not even all in the same city for LA county. I thought this was ridiculous.

Back at work, things were enjoyable. He had volunteered his time to be an assistant coach on the basketball team. *Basketball was his first love, after all.* The team practiced at a high school gym in inner-city Los Angeles, and I'll never forget the day that he returned home from work to report that someone had broken into the car during practice and had taken his briefcase. All of his receipts were in the briefcase, and he was utterly defeated. We had started going through so many of these negative experiences with his baby momma that we decided that we had no choice but to stay positive and keep pushing forward because we knew that he was doing the right thing. We always believed that things happened for a reason, and we tried to figure out what the lesson was in that particular incident. Ultimately, we had to accept that God allows some things to happen and doesn't necessarily reveal the reason why during the time that you think you need to understand, and that we just have to live with these events.

Although every one of his family members and many of hers knew that he had supported their child since her birth, from the used car he purchased for her so that she'd have some transportation with the baby, to the refrigerator that his family pitched in to buy while he was in school for her apartment, to the money orders that he had sent directly to his baby momma's mother to assure that she would get them, to the extra job that he had taken on just to send the checks to her while carrying a full course load in college — none of that meant anything to the courts. If you are in a similar situation, make copies of all of your receipts. You never know when you may have to use them.

The District Attorney told my boyfriend that he was supposed to be giving her the maximum child support while he was a fulltime student, although there was proof on record that he was never served, that in fact the form was sent to the baby momma's girlfriend's house. The court said that he was even supposed to be paying the maximum child support to her even while she lived with him. In a nutshell, they told him that he now owed over $14,000 when his daughter was just around four years old because he had never paid anything. I know, you are asking why he didn't get an attorney. We did after a while, but to be honest, in the beginning, we thought an attorney would be too expensive and that this silly case was cut and dried because he had the truth on his side. We were sadly mistaken. The first attorney that we ended up retaining made a bigger mess of the situation. After this, we were afraid to trust anyone. My boyfriend disagreed with the DA and ended up getting the amount owed down to just over $7000. He couldn't believe that he was negotiating to pay back money that he never owed in the first place. His baby momma needed to get him back, and because the courts had allowed him joint custody and he had obviously moved on with his life, she had found a way. She was right in her assumption, he was angry, but now nothing she could do would ever earn her his love or respect again. He also wasn't going to give up on his right to be in his daughter's life no matter who didn't like it.

REAL TALK 9

**Hell hath no fury like a woman scorned.
PERIOD.**

CHAPTER TEN
Resilient but Human

Despite dealing with the negative fallout that came along with being forced to deal with negative people, my boyfriend and I managed to recognize our blessings. The battle to spend time with his daughter went on and on in addition to the battle with the courts. We decided to continue educating ourselves as we were dedicated to the idea of being lifelong learners. We worked hard to show those around us that young people could be successful in love and life if they too worked hard and committed themselves to progress. We both understood that we were working at jobs that would serve as stepping stones to where we were ultimately trying to be in life, and that there was no prescription for how we were to proceed for that time in our lives. We met many good people along the way, and we were showered with love and affection from our families. My family loved him, and his family, with *very few exceptions*, loved me. Nevertheless, there were exceptions.

We had been able to focus on our lives together without interruption or too much socializing. The majority of our friends were still in northern California, and because we had relocated, we were able to plan our fun time with them. We both had very close-knit circles of friends, and sometimes, such circles aren't good for blossoming relationships, especially with men. Men need to hang out with, be like, and impress their friends, which can be a little overwhelming for a relationship. That's not to say that some women don't know how to put their friendships in the proper perspective when in a relationship, but I'd say that overall we are better at it than men.

All of the years that our lives had been intertwined, including all of the experiences both good and bad, seemed to consummate the next step for us. We didn't talk too much about it let alone make plans. Things were just falling into place and seemed right. It had not been easy, but we agreed that we felt a spiritual connection to each other that demanded we stay unified and supportive of one another, friends and partners together. The spiritual connection between two people is just a feeling, knowing that you are being led by a Higher Power and embracing that feeling. I believe we were linked together, and it was truly like someone else decided how the cards would fall for us — but only after strengthening us with difficult experiences so that we could grow as individuals and as a couple. Keep in mind that you cannot be happy in a relationship or for anyone else if you are not happy with yourself.

I'll never forget his resolution on our first New Year's Eve celebration together after moving to southern California. He resolved that we would be engaged the following year. That next Christmas Eve, the ring was in hand and we made the commitment to marry each other.

We were on our way to have dinner with loved ones when he decided to make me angry. I don't remember what he started to talk about, but I was not in the mood to have an argument. He made me mad. He was picking out things to argue about, and I was so unsuspecting, which was right where he wanted me to be. After he finished telling me something that he didn't like, he countered with something that he loved about me and shared that these were the reasons why he wanted me to be his wife. He pulled out the ring box and got down on his knee and asked, "Will you marry me?" My emotions had gone from anger to confusion to pure joy. The small grin that I'd had once I realized that he was setting me up had turned into a big smile, and I said yes, wrapping my arms around him and jumping on him with immense excitement. Now to many of you, I know this doesn't sound too romantic, but it was enough to make me happy and it worked for us. When it works for you, you'll know.

He and I made the move to Los Angeles just days before Christmas. We left late in the evening and began the journey to our new life together. It was long and treacherous as we drove all night. I was in my car, and he drove the moving truck with all of our belongings and towing his car. We stopped midway, took a nap together, woke up a short time later, and continued on our journey. We made it safely and without incident early the next morning, both exhausted. We woke up refreshed, and we knew that we could make it through anything, that this was just the first test in a series of many to come.

Although he and I had agreed not to do anything

major for one another for the Christmas holiday when we first moved to LA, he had bought me a special gift he would call a "promise ring." A year later, he would be replacing that promise ring with a token of his actual promise — an engagement ring. We had never even gone out and looked for rings nor talked about what I wanted. He went out with his dad one afternoon without providing me with any real details as to where he was going, but did exceptionally well picking out the most beautiful and perfect ring for me. I couldn't have asked for a better token of his affection. His family members were happy for us the next day, Christmas, and everyone wanted to see my engagement ring and became excited about a wedding in the future.

My boyfriend and I had not spent much time talking about the wedding, but up to that point, we had spent ample time making plans for our future together. The wedding is not nearly as important as your life together, but I urge you not to get caught up with living as his wife when you are not officially. The ceremony takes on average about 35 minutes to complete and is but a tenth of a fraction of the time it will take you to build a life together. Don't get married because everyone else is or because you think you better take advantage of an opportunity. Marry someone because you truly love them and want to build a life together. Someone wrote, "Marry the right person. This decision alone will determine 90% of your happiness or misery." If you don't believe this statement, ask around and the truth shall surface.

We took several months to actually plan our wedding day, and in the meantime, we continued to work through the day-to-day struggles and life lessons that continued to meet us. His daughter had now gotten the chance to be a part of our lives, and despite all of the negative energy that had transpired before her, she managed to be very sweet and innocent and loving. She loved and accepted me with the most refreshing spirit. She and her dad loved spending time together, and I loved to watch them enjoy each other. In a weird way, it was like he was beginning to relive some of the relationship he lost with his mother. He was so young, around age six, when she was killed that he had an emotional gap that his daughter seemed to fit right into. She adored her dad, and I'd hoped that she would one day know all that he was going through just to have the chance to love her up close. She looked a lot like him, and according to his family members, she was a lot like his mother. She was very observant, and I only hoped that none of this negativity would ruin her bright and innocent spirit. Kids are resilient, but they are still human, so think about what you expose them to. Think back to your own childhood, and I'm sure you will still remember certain difficult incidents.

We were always pleased when we got the chance to spend family time with his daughter. By now, he and I had lots of time to grow together with each other, and I felt comfortable that the natural progression of our relationship toward family would unite us. Things were still difficult for me though because I had a hard time accepting all of the things that were happening with his daughter's mom. A few years had gone by, and she was still so angry that it was sad. I know this might sound strange, but I truly felt sorry for her. She seemed to be unable to release the anger and misery that she was feeling for all of those years toward us. I had hoped that we would be able to be "adult" about things, but that wasn't going to happen any time soon. I knew that she would be angry in the beginning, and as a woman, I understood that, but I couldn't believe that she had still not let that go. There is nothing you can do about another person being unhappy in their own life. Because his daughter was a part of her mom's life, we prayed for them, prayed that his daughter's mom would find some sort of peace and happiness in her own life, enough so that she would stop trying to ruin our happiness and enough so that she would put their child above all.

To date, she and I had never had a conversation. What did she expect from him? I was trying to be the bigger person, but hey, I was happy. I had my man and he had some kind of relationship with his baby girl. As a woman, I knew that nothing made the baby momma angrier than the sight of me, and so I pushed — I couldn't help myself. I wasn't nasty, but I was always well put together when she saw me, cheerful and beautiful just to push the limit because I could. I never said anything to her, but I was obviously happy, and that alone made her angry. I knew that she felt like I had taken something that belonged to her. I know how this goes. Even if she never believed that she would have him again, once the baby came, she just knew that she would always have a place in his heart. She knew that she could get from him whatever she wanted, but she never saw me in the picture. I thought for a while that I could be bitter like that in my own life if things had gone differently, never finding love, but I wasn't willing to settle and instead fought for what I wanted. Love prevailed because my heart was open.

Although there had been many times that we both had gone to court or to the child's school for activities, she could not let her feelings go. She usually had a girlfriend with her, someone who was also a baby momma, to help ease her pain, I guess. No one really wants to be alone. I only wondered whether any of them ever tried to convince her to choose the higher road. I'll assume they didn't because they themselves were also in similar boats. Because they went to high school together, he knew many of her friends along with their stories.

Court ordered time with my boyfriend's daughter included every other weekend, along with a few hours in the middle of the week and every other holiday. There were a few exceptions around birthdays and Mother's Day and Father's Day, but much of the schedule was probably quite typical. The Christmas holiday schedule had turned out to be the most difficult to follow. One year, he'd be allowed time on Christmas Eve until 12 noon and vice versa. Once school started, and after more court dates and more lawyers, the order would change again. However, these more permanent changes would not occur until after the "big fallout."

One year on Christmas, we had his daughter with us and decided to defy the court order for a day so that we could spend time together on a short vacation because our start time got pushed back. We honestly didn't have plans to keep her for the extra day until her mom decided to have her ready for us to pick her up closer to 4 p.m. rather than at 12 p.m. Our time was obviously cut a little short. We knew that we would now be guilty of the same thing that she had been doing all along, but we figured that, because the courts had done nothing about her abuse of her rights, maybe they'd do nothing if we kept her the extra day. The girl's mom called around the time that she was due back and was told that we would not be bringing her back until the following return day. She was angry, to say the least. You see, now it didn't seem so fair because my boyfriend was doing to her what she had been doing over and over.

We had a wonderful time on our mini-vacation, and upon returning home, we immediately unloaded a few items out of the car and headed over to drop her off at her mother's. It was his normal practice to call his daughter's mom once he was close so that she would make her way out of her apartment and meet their daughter at the gate. He did make the call, but when we arrived, she wasn't alone. She had her two brothers and her boyfriend at the time waiting outside in their car. Once we pulled up and gave goodbye hugs and kisses, as my boyfriend walked around the car with his daughter's hand in his, these guys rushed out of the car lunged forward to attack him. He had recognized them immediately, and he let his daughter's hand go, pushing her out of the way. She began screaming and crying. Of course, she recognized her uncles, but she was unaware of why they were trying to attack her dad. Her mom came rushing out of the gate and grabbed their daughter, taking her upstairs while her friends came out of the gate.

In the meantime, I had jumped out of the driver's seat, and my brother, who was in the backseat, was met by a man with a nine millimeter handgun as he tried to climb out of the car. My boyfriend ran down the street in an attempt to draw her brothers' attention to him while giving us a chance to leave. He did not know, however, that there was another guy with a gun and a couple of her girlfriends there who had come out to attack me. I turned around to find someone I had never seen before directly in front of me, and she started to swing. I swung in an attempt to hit back with the one good arm that I had, and then dropped to the ground to try and cover myself. I had no idea what was coming, but I knew that it would be over soon and that I'd survive whatever it was.

My boyfriend came running back down the street in disbelief when he saw the guy with the gun trying to break out the car window. By this time, the neighbors had called the police. Everyone was outside now. One brother had gotten away while the other had gotten arrested along with the guy who had the gun. Her friends were trying to drive off with his daughter and their children in the car when the police stopped them and made them all get out. His daughter was covered up in the backseat, hiding with the other children and crying her eyes out. They made her get out, and my boyfriend grabbed her, telling her that everything was going to be okay. She was all of four years old at the time. That night ended with us going home in anger and disgust, his daughter going home with her maternal grandmother, and baby momma and her pack going to jail.

Although things had gotten really bad, we knew that God was with us that night. My brother had a very short temper at the time, and he had been shot before so he had gotten used to carrying a gun. However, he had gotten in the car with us to drop my boyfriend's daughter off and left his gun in his car. Praise God, who protected us from what could have been murder that night. Being from big families and all being from inner cities, this could have gotten so much worse. My boyfriend knew where all of the attackers lived. He knew them personally. My family was ready to jump, and so was his family, but everyone kicked back instead, including my very anxious brother, and waited for my boyfriend to make the call. He slept on it, and although he was murderously angry and anxiously awaiting the opportunity to see either of her brothers individually, there was one thing more important than all of that — his daughter. It took a long time to get over that incident, but we did and we were blessed.

We went to court, and my boyfriend was granted temporary custody. He picked his daughter up from school, providing the school with the court papers, and they reluctantly let her go with him but they called her mom right away. The girl's mother rushed to the school before going to the police station. My boyfriend then provided the police with the paperwork, and they told her she would need to deal with the courts. I'm sure what followed had to be the longest couple of months in her life. She was only able to have a supervised visit with her daughter, and she finally had the chance to see what it was like to be without her. We tried to keep things as normal as possible for my boyfriend's daughter, realizing that she would miss her mother. We explained to her that her mom had done something bad but that things would get better and she would be able to see her mom again.

We went back to court after the temporary custody order. Baby momma told the judge that nothing had happened to grant the custody change and that she was not arrested. We provided the judge with the arrest record, proving her a liar under oath, and the judge still returned custody to her. She had been evicted from her apartment and was staying with a friend until finding another place, but the courts ignored that as well. I could not believe it. The judge ordered a court-appointed agency to complete visitations with the child while she was at each of her parent's homes, which didn't take place until a few months later. By this time, her mom had of course had time to find another place.

The court ordered another evaluation several months later. This time the report had been completely turned around. The same questions were answered with obvious coaching. His daughter had substantiated everything we had told the courts the first time, and we did not talk to her ahead of time except to tell her that she should tell them the truth. But at the second hearing, my boyfriend's daughter completely changed her story and I was livid. At that time, I was so hurt. I could not believe the things that she said about her dad to these people, but even worse, I knew that her mom had coached her. It was that obvious. Still, with all that he had done for his baby girl, I never thought she would lie on her dad like that. She was no older than six, and I could not believe that a mother would put their own child in this predicament all for the sake of revenge. He was so disappointed and heartbroken, but he knew that his child was innocent in all of this. This was a hard pill for me to swallow, but as we had been doing over and over, we toughed it out and made sure not to express our complete disgust for his daughter's mom in front of his baby girl. We knew that her mom loved her but was just more committed to her own anger than to her child's happiness. Life goes on. We could only pray that one day she would heal and realize what she was doing to her daughter.

REAL TALK 10

Situations like this are very serious, and it amazes me that there is not more support for people in these circumstances. The children are devastated by these constant problems between their parents, and indeed, children are often kept from people who love them. The trouble that an angry ex will go through just to get revenge is sad. I have witnessed a man trying to love his child without pursuing a relationship with her mother, and I have never been so embarrassed by the actions of another woman. I cannot express enough my disappointment and lack of confidence in the child custody and child support systems, in the state of CA at least. I'm sure that not every situation turns out this badly, but I have heard countless stories by numerous individuals about this very thing. For the children, as adults, we must come to a better resolution. If you are in a situation like this, and you know that your children are suffering because of your actions, please allow them the love that they are due. A child is not blind, and if they have a parent who is not a good person or does bad things, they will address it with that parent in their own time. It is not your place to stand in the way of your child's relationship with their other parent unless you are certain that they will harm the child. There are of course extreme exceptions, but in cases of your own pain or misery, please don't make the child suffer. Although I know that there are bad fathers out there, I am addressing the women right now. We seem to get this automatic acceptance as a good mother when we have a child, but in truth, not every woman is a good mother. We cannot take this for granted. Our family structures need both parents — that's why it takes two to make a child. These cycles repeat themselves if we don't end them, and we all suffer. I realize that some of you may not agree with me but we are all entitled to our opinions. I had to get this off of my heart. Now, back to relationships...

CHAPTER ELEVEN
Checklist

By this time, my boyfriend and I had gotten used to life's challenges. Even though we expected them for growth or personal and spiritual development, we never knew how God was going to choose to teach us what life was about. We had lots of incredible things going on with our careers and educational paths, and life was full for us. We also had each other. We had true love and that made life worth living. Some of you may think that I had all of the reason in the world to walk away from my boyfriend and all of this drama, but the truth is that I never even thought about it. I wanted him because he was beautiful to me. He made my heart smile. He had gone through so many tough things early in his life, and I thought that his life should be grand from then on. If I could help him achieve that, I was going to. Although during college he was a selfish, rotten (fill in the blank) to me, he was just being a man. Again, I remind you that this is my story and that I do not recommend anyone do what I did. However, I encourage each of you to know as much as you can about what you are getting yourselves into with any potential partner. Not every woman can go through all of that unnecessary drama for a man, and not everyone should. I never had any intention of going through the drama myself, but ultimately, I chose to love a man who had a child and a baby momma. He didn't deliberately ask for this drama either, but those early actions, hurting all those women, were coming back to haunt him. It's just a shame that a woman would use her own child to try to make a man feel the pain.

My boyfriend wasn't the only one with a problem that would cause us much grief. We would soon be called to answer one of the toughest challenges yet. I was taking the next test on my career path, and he was taking classes as well. Together, we were busy planning our wedding and making life plans when everything came to a screeching halt. While going down my checklist for the wedding, there was one thing that I knew I needed to do. I had gone to the doctor's office for a regular scheduled appointment, but this time I needed to ask them about this unusual little lump that had appeared on my chest. They checked it out and told me that they were sure it was nothing due to my age and family history, and they sent me on my way. I didn't think much more about it until the lump continued to grow and I still had no idea what it was. I'd had a lump on my neck a few years earlier that turned out to be nothing, and so I was pretty sure that this would be the same.

I went to see my regular doctor again, and she decided that I should go to another office to have an ultrasound since the lump had not gone away yet. There was no pain or anything, but just the fact that it was there was enough to cause some concern. I went to the next office, which didn't do ultrasounds, as it turned out, and so as

CHECKLIST

you could guess I was getting a little impatient with the whole process. They sent me to yet another office to have the ultrasound done, and finally I could check one more item off of my list. I was running all over town getting decoration ideas and invitations out and the host of other things that are usually part of wedding planning when I got the call from the clinic that my test results came back abnormal. They asked me to return as soon as possible for more tests. Ultimately, I was diagnosed with breast cancer. I was 27 years old, had no breast cancer throughout my maternal family line, and I barely had breasts.

I didn't have time to slow down though. I was getting married in less than a week and nothing was going to stop me from being the most beautiful bride marrying the most terrific man imaginable. I held my head up and had the most perfect wedding just a few days later. Our wedding day was filled with our family and friends, many of whom had witnessed our relationship from the beginning. Ours was a relationship that beat seemingly insurmountable odds, and the marriage felt so right. We came up with our own vows and our vision was a reality on that very special day.

It was important for us to have a theme for our wedding, one that spelled out who we were. For us, love and life together were the most important messages, and from the colors to the song selections, everything needed to be perfect. We chose the most amazing apple-red with platinum. It was no surprise to most that I chose red, but I did not choose it for the reasons that some may have guessed. This apple-red was not just any red, it was the most beautiful expression of passion in a color that I had seen, and therefore I knew it was perfect for our big day. We took just as much care in selecting our bridesmaids and groomsmen. We needed to decide how many we were going to have because we both had so many people that we loved and were close to. We are both from large families, and so we had a combination of family members and friends, sorority sisters and fraternity brothers. We agreed on a total of eighteen bridesmaids and groomsmen including our Maids of Honor and Best Men. Everything about our wedding needed to express who we were. We wanted to share love with everyone there and hoped that they too would find the kind of love we now knew if they had not already. I strongly suggest, ladies, that you make your wedding your own. There are some things that are tradition, of course, but be sure to express your love and the life you have planned together to the world. Remember, you should be planning to do this one time, so go all out.

Our wedding favors were little platinum plastic hearts held together with a red ribbon. Once they were opened, there was a message inside, lines from one of my favorite India Arie songs: "I close my eyes and I think of all the things I want to see. Now that I've opened up my heart, I know that anything I want can be." I was listening to an India Arie CD and was so moved at the time by her messages of faith and hope that we also decided "Strength, Courage and Wisdom" would be the theme for our wedding. Although my fiancé and I felt that it was meant for us to be together, we knew that there was no way to predict success in marriage, and so we spent several weeks in

CHECKLIST

marriage counseling, and it was great. Our counselor was so gracious and thorough that we knew we were blessed for having her. We also spent time with our spiritual advisor and financial advisor just making sure that we were considering the right things and that all of our I's were dotted and T's crossed. Throughout all of this, I never felt worried about whether or not we were meant to be.

We each had celebrations with our friends the night before the wedding. He enjoyed a bachelor party and I enjoyed a flavorful bachelorette. We both had a great time with our friends and all of the festivities that were planned for us. For those of you who might be wondering, we never talked to each other about the details of the events and it has never led to a problem between us. We were each glad that the other had fun and we were not concerned about what that fun included. I've seen this topic on talk shows and wondered why it would need to come up after marriage. If you feel the need to question what your partner would do at the bachelor party, that's not your only reservation and you should really be sure that marriage is the right thing for the two of you.

Many of our family members and friends made it to celebrate our special day with us from northern California, and a few flew in from a little farther away. We appreciated everyone for making the trip and being there with us. If you didn't know before, after something like a wedding, you will know who your true friends are.

Music was very important to us, and we wanted to make sure that we chose the songs that translated our feelings best. We had been trying over and over to pick the perfect song for our bridal party to enter to, when one day my fiancé called me with the one. "Nothing Even Matters" by Lauryn Hill featuring DeAngelo. I loved the song, but as with all of our selections, I needed to listen to it to make sure that it didn't say anything inappropriate. It worked perfectly. I still remember all of the song choices from the wedding to the reception. I would walk out to my male cousin singing a beautiful, heartfelt rendition of "Still in Love" by Brian McKnight. It was so sweet. My smile was ear to ear as my father proudly walked me down the aisle. I remember looking at my fiancé in his all-white tux next to his beautiful dark skin, wearing a confident smile and waiting for me at the altar.

Everything was working out as we had planned, but we did have the set back of his daughter being kept away from the wedding by her mother, which I'm sure is no surprise to any of you. We had planned for her to be the flower girl as she so anxiously wanted to be, but at the last minute, her mom decided to mysteriously disappear with her. Although we both had family members who would have happily filled in, we decided not to replace her and proceeded with our plans. Everything else was in place from the ring bearer to the person who carried the creatively decorated broom. For those who may not be aware, the broom symbolizes our ancestors' commitment to marriage because African Americans were denied marriage early in American history. We honored them by jumping the broom at the end of our ceremony.

My bridesmaids were lovely in the dresses that were specifically designed for them, each wearing a dress with

CHECKLIST

a different design made out of the exact same apple-red fabric. My cousin's fiancé and I had come up with the designs for these dresses and she made them all. I loved the idea of each woman being beautiful in her own way, just as they were in my heart. The platinum shoes and nylons and sparkling jewelry pieces were the perfect accessories. My dress, which I designed, was made by a wonderful and incredibly talented woman — and it was stunning. I had a vision of something chic yet luxurious, and she brought the vision to life, and in fact, the wedding dress was even more beautiful than I had imagined. From my impeccable, corn-rowed hair to the shoes made for a queen, from my flawless makeup to my fancy little handbag and veil, my look flowed together beautifully on my special day. And, of course, to top it off was my fabulous platinum and diamond wedding ring set. I was determined to savor the moment, and the pictures and videos provided us with a lifetime of enjoyment of our special day..

It was also very important to us to add a few things that were symbolic specifically of our relationship. Because he suffered the loss of his mother so many years prior, we reserved a seat for her by placing her name on a chair in the front row at our wedding. One of my best friends and bridesmaids read a beautiful poem that encompassed our theme: "Strength, Courage and Wisdom." And our very special first dance song was "Time Will Reveal" by El Debarge. It was the perfect song. This wedding seemed like such a long time coming and there were so many trials we had to survive, and this song expressed that love conquers all. We had first become connected to this song about two years before getting married. It came on the radio while we were at work, and I remember my boyfriend writing a few of the words on a sheet of paper and giving it to me. There was no song more perfect for our first dance.

Remember, ladies, that the measure of a man and woman's love isn't about how perfect the wedding is — the true test of the relationship is time itself. We had a fabulous time celebrating our love with our loved ones, but the true test had only just begun.

CHECKLIST

REAL TALK 11

Don't be afraid to be tested, especially when it comes to God's plan for you. You need to know as much as you can about one another, especially those things that will indeed affect your decision making and your life together. Know what you are getting yourself into so that you'll know what you need to get yourself out of. Listen to your heart and spirit, which tells you when things are not right as well as when you have all that you need for things to be right, and then be honest with yourself and with each other. Remember that your relationship isn't about everyone else, but about you two. Always remember that the wedding is the easy part, so have fun.

CHAPTER TWELVE
Why Not Me?

We knew there was adversity to come, but what was new? We'd buckle down and handle it like we had handled every other difficult situation. I always knew that I was special, and now I knew for sure. God was ready to do His thing with me, and I was ready for it. I had all of the love and support in place that I needed to deal with the cancer and to be comfortable that greater things were to come for me. I was ready for the wakeup call to live my life with every ounce of passion I could muster. I had experienced the most beautiful wedding a girl could have along with a fabulous Jamaican honeymoon. I was back at home, and it was time to tackle the next major step. I would start chemotherapy soon, and just two weeks after that, I started writing my first book, *I Want It Now! Analyze Where You Are in Life, Discover Your Passion and Achieve Ultimate Happiness*. I figured I'd better make my mark because nothing in life was promised.

I mentioned in the previous chapter that I had use of one arm for a while during the time that the "big fall out" occurred. I had a mastectomy about a week before the Christmas Holiday, and with everything going on, I knew that I was in the place that God had personally selected for me. I was truly grateful that it was me instead of my mother or grandmother, my sisters or friends. I felt I could handle this illness and all that came along with it. I wasn't ready to lose all of my hair, but I managed to stay cute during the process, and if you saw me today, you'd never know it was gone. I was on a mission. I was positive, and I felt so blessed to have my husband by my side, as committed to me as I was to him. I know that things would not have been the same without him. He went to every doctor's appointment with me and sat there for hours as I received chemotherapy. He loved me when I lost all of my hair, *and he still thought I was sexy*, took care of me the days I didn't feel so well, and took me out when I wanted to socialize. He encouraged me to push forward with everything that I wanted to do. He walked by my side.

I had the support of so many loved ones during this time, but it was actually harder for me to tell them what I was going through than to actually go through it. I didn't want them to hurt for me or feel sorry for me. I'm sure that many were having a difficult time knowing that I was going through something as serious as cancer, as many had never been this close to someone with the disease before. Up to that point, my life seemed ideal. Things were working out according to plan in many others eyes, but I knew that this was just a part of God's plan as well. I had always strived for success, and I was the type of person who usually prevailed when it came to my goals. A few people automatically equated cancer with death, and so they were really scared for me. One thing that I knew through all of this was that God was not going to take me away this early. I was 27 years old, and I knew that my time on this earth was not yet served, that I would not yet be taken from my loved ones or the many others in the world that I had not yet had the chance to inspire. My husband had also been dealt such an unfair hand of cards that I knew God wouldn't take me from him just yet. He never seemed to doubt that life was beginning for me, just as I had not.

I was in a good place with my support base, and I had visitors regularly. I could rest when necessary, and I even had family members and friends fly down to support me for a few days here and there. I was treated the same as always by all of them, like I could do anything that I wanted, and yet there was always a concern for how I was feeling — and this was different for me. I was even able to get the adults comfortable with looking at my bald head once I lost my hair and still continue on as normal, even though it was different than any look I had ever had before. I say the adults because I would not allow the children to see me that way. I didn't want them to be afraid.

I remember the night that my husband and I decided to shave off what was left of my hair together. I had been losing my hair little by little, each time that I ran a comb through it. Of course, my hair was the longest it had been since childhood prior to my losing it all. I anticipated the loss, but I could never really prepare for it. I would comb through it in disbelief as handfuls would fall out every single time. My hair was very thick so it took a lot before it was thin enough to see my scalp through it, but one day, my scalp felt tender and sore. It was like someone had been pulling on my hair all day and I needed a resolution. I decided that I would run a hot bath and have my husband massage my shoulders and my scalp while washing my hair for me. As soon as it had gotten wet, it tangled up like a couple of large dread locks. I was flabbergasted. Once I had gotten out of the tub, I knew what I had to do. I grabbed the clippers and handed them to my husband to shave me bald. In a weird sort of way, it was liberating. I had gotten down on my knees and rested my arms on the sink so that he could see everything. If I was going to be bald, it needed to be done right. I felt better knowing that I wouldn't have to watch my hair continue to fall out. As I looked at myself in the mirror, I let a few tears drop, and I remember wondering how it would be when it grew back. The funniest thing about my new look was that I still had sun tan lines in my head from the cornrows I had worn during my wedding and honeymoon. This was a sight to see in combination with seeing myself bald for the first time. As I looked forward, I knew one thing. I still looked good and my husband confirmed it.

All you ladies, whether or not you have any risk factors for cancer, know that you are beautiful inside and out. Be comfortable that, if you ever had to look at yourself in the mirror with no hair or anything else to shield who you really are, you need to be happy with what you see. There is nothing to hide your insecurity when you are a bald woman, trust me.

There were a lot of things that were difficult, but of course, there were some advantages as well. I didn't have to shave for a while in places that I normally did, like underneath my arms, my legs or even my eyebrows because the hair stopped growing during chemotherapy. I had baby-soft skin too, and that wasn't so bad.

My brother had gone with me on one of my first trips to the beauty supply store for a wig. I tried on so many stylish wigs and was quite impressed with the choices that were available. Many were similar to a few of my old hair styles as a matter of fact. The wigs were all lengths and colors, and that was fun. My brother kept bringing different wigs for me to try on, and together we'd look at each one and give it a thumbs up or down. We left with a few wigs, and even a couple of nifty little hats that, once combined with the wig, made it look like my real hair. I've always been very particular about my hair, and this didn't change in the wig shop. The good thing was that I changed my hair regularly so a new look for me was nothing new.

I'll never forget the day we went to the comedy club. My husband and I had taken one of my girlfriends along with us, and we had a good time. I remember looking around the club and noticing the overwhelming number of women who had some form of fake hair. There were wigs, weaves, braids with extensions, and so I felt right in place with my cute new wig. The funny thing was that, for the first time, I wondered how many of them were perhaps wearing a wig because they too had been stricken with cancer or some other illness. It had never occurred to me before. I would have probably never noticed, or I might have written it off as the latest trend in hairstyles. Amazing how life experiences can change your views. I even went to my ten-year class reunion that year, and no one even noticed that I was a woman undergoing chemotherapy. We had a nice time reminiscing about our high school times, and I marveled at how I would have never expected to have breast cancer then, especially not a short ten years later.

God ordered my steps for me just as He does for all of us. He placed all of those that I would need in my life around me so that I would be victorious. With God's help, my husband and I fought the cancer right out of my system. At this point, I am cancer free and I am happy in love and life.

There were still a few things that had not happened for me yet, however. I didn't know whether or not I would be able to have children. I had never been pregnant before, and I wondered at how the chemo might affect me in this regard. As you could imagine, I was concerned about this. My husband, who looked forward to having more children one day, told me not to worry. He assured me that my health and my life were more important than whether or not I could have children. My paternal grandmother, who also survived breast cancer, used to say, "If you are going to pray, don't worry, and if you are going to worry, don't pray." We prayed about the possibility of having children one day, and the matter was left in God's hands. I didn't know at the time if He wanted me to be a mother for there was so much work in the world for me to do. The task at hand required me to take care of me, and that was something that I was up for. My career was ready for a shift. My relationship was off to a great start, and I was on my way to fulfilling my passion. Life could only get better, right?

REAL TALK 12

I challenge you to consider whether or not the person you are in a relationship with now, or want to be in a relationship with, will be there for you in the event that something tragic and unexpected were to happen to you. Would they love you and support you the way that you would need? You don't need to ask him because you know in your heart. If you cannot answer yes, you know what you need to do. Most of the time in relationships, we know what we need to do, but what it really comes down to is being strong enough to **DO** it.

Be careful how you determine what love means to you. Love doesn't cost a thing yet it can cost you everything.
—*Forrest D.L. Hightower*

Part Three
the Love

CHAPTER THIRTEEN
Music Was My First Love...

Since we're talking about love here, I have to let you know when I knew that this was love, when the connection was made for me. I'm going to take you back for a minute, but join me on this ride for this was the remarkable Aha! moment for me that Oprah talks about as it pertained to l-o-v-e.

I had driven down to San Francisco to meet a few of my girlfriends for some social activity. After hanging out for most of the day and enjoying myself, the time had finally come for me to go home. My work schedule at the juvenile hall sometimes required me to work on Saturdays, and due to this schedule, I had driven down alone. The city was only about 45 minutes away, and therefore I didn't mind.

I am a music lover, and so I used the time to myself to think and listen to some of my favorite songs. Still to this day, I sing away while I am in the car and "my song" comes on, especially one that I am really feeling at the moment. And no, I don't have to be in the car alone. My favorite music is R&B and Hip Hop, and so I went back and forth between the FM Hip Hop and R&B radio station and my CDs listening for good songs.

I had begun thinking about my friend and wondering what he was doing. Although I had gone out with my girls and tried to fill my time with interesting things to do, you could probably guess that, by the end of the day, my mind would end up on him. I started feeling sad because I was on my way home to be alone again while my friend was out doing who knows what. I felt tired and sad that I had not been able to replace him with someone more deserving of my heart. This realization had taken me to a melancholy place. At the time, the Lauryn Hill CD *Miseducation of Lauryn Hill* that I was listening to soothed my pain. Music has the tremendous power to change your mood, even to relieve stress.

I had become pretty familiar with the CD, learning most of the words and getting so pumped up at many of the messages that she put out in her songs, but it was more than just her words that made the difference for me. Her voice sounded like I felt, strong yet sensitive, soulful — powerful and yet powerless. Something about her voice made me listen to my inner self. Finally, "Tell Him," the last song on her CD, came on and I was pouring out the words in my best singing voice, thinking about how much I meant these words for my friend and how I wish he could hear my heart speaking to him when it clicked along with the second verse of the song, that she was talking about God not a man. Tears dropped from my eyes, and from that moment, I knew. I finally understood. God was love, and here I thought it was my friend. No person has that kind of power unless we give it to them, but God allows us to know a love so beautiful that it transcends the human spirit. God is love.

REAL TALK 13

There is no method, no step-by-step for how to know you have found him. For starters though, you should begin looking in the right place — up. God is the Answer, and I know this for sure. He's trying to tell you, but He may have to make a way through and around many other situations first. If you are tired of hurting because of bad decisions or bad choices in men, get in touch with your heart. Listen to your spirit. The answer is there.

CHAPTER FOURTEEN
Get It Together

Although it has taken many years and experiences, I can say that I have been fairly happy with my choices in life and in love. My husband has been hard working and very supportive. I have made solid educational choices, and I have been exposed to many different career opportunities. I have friendships and kinship with a very loving group of people. I have had the chance to learn more about myself and my husband, and together, we have been challenged in major ways, including those that encouraged our love, growth, and our increasing strength together. I now know that, although many of the experiences that I have gone through in life have been difficult, God was only preparing me for the work He had in store for me later. My work is only just beginning, and although my relationship is strong and solid at this time, all I can definitely speak about is "now," because there are no definitives in love.

My husband and I have prospered together. We have tried to express our gratitude for the many wonderful blessings as well as the support and validation that we received through it all. We are strong as a unit, and all of the things that we have gotten through together only confirms this. We have been blessed.

Though I believe these things to be true for us, this translation is being shared from my own understanding of our relationship and his perception could be different, which is one of the lessons that I have learned since being married. This is also another reason why it is important to know who you are and what you want apart from your relationship. One of the many things that I have learned from my own relationship experience is that couples may fall off course without both parties being aware of it, and so it is very important to always communicate honestly. Not everyone is good at talking, and in most couples, one person is usually dominant in the communication area. Therefore, write a letter, use email, send text messages, or whatever you have to do to keep the lines open and the communication effective. There are too many communication methods available nowadays that make it easier to say what you really feel, so be sure to try some form that works for you.

In successful relationships, couples should be unified in their understanding of their partnership — you should be on the same page. It is important to share your perceptions with one another. I came to my own understanding about many things while being single, including how relationships are supposed to be, but since becoming part of couple, I now have to understand in concert with my husband in order to be successful in the relationship with him, even if that understanding points out our differences. In real life, even though it is the best thing to do, such mutual understanding is very difficult to achieve. By the way, understanding together does not mean agreeing on everything. Looking back, the time that I spent alone without a man in my life was such a short time. If you are single now, and especially if you are without children, use this time and space to really develop who you are and what you want. Once things start rolling, you never get that time back. When you are in a relationship with someone, a partnership, you do not have as much time to give to you. The time I spent alone seemed like forever then, but time is like the enemy when your heart is longing for someone or something that you do not have, whether or not it is something that you are ready for.

As I mentioned earlier, things were going well, but of course that did not mean that the work was over. In fact, the work was only just beginning. In my case, it took a lot to get what I wanted, but no matter the effort to get to this stage, it takes even more to maintain a solid and honest, happy and thriving marriage. I often hear people say that relationships are hard, especially marriage, but I never really understood why. Today, I personally think that the reason is because the only person you can control, even in a relationship, is you. The only feelings you control are your own. You can't make someone happy because you are happy. You can't make someone get it because you do. After all of the things that we do to get into relationships, we are tested on the lessons we were supposed to be learning all along. We are tested on who we are, what we believe, what we will stand for and what we won't; and trust me, the tests are a lot harder once you have a partner in your life, someone you believe should pass because you passed. What do you do when your partner does not pass? Be sure that you are being true to yourself so that this transition into a relationship, sharing your life with someone else, will not be so difficult.

I once heard that everything in life is either a reward or a test, and I wonder how many rewards or tests one might be given. Interestingly, I also wonder how many times we get the same test. We may be tested together or individually once we are in relationships because together we make up the couple. However, we remain two individual parts that are supposed to be strong and one part should be able to stand when the other part is weak. Just as a chain is only as strong as its weakest link, however, a couple can only be as strong as its weakest half. It is crucial that couples are at similar levels of strength and clarity, however, because there are only two halves. If one is rising and the other is descending, the two will go in the direction of the stronger half, and negative energy will prevail over positive energy because that is the easier path. We each have to be sure that we are learning lessons in addition to those our partner represents, growing spiritually in addition to your partner. Do not assume that because you see something clearly your partner also sees the situation clearly. You might be tested together, but the grade may be based on how well each of you did on your own, but what do you do when the test comes through your partner's weakness? If you don't know who you are, you are going to be faced with the most extreme doubt in your ability to pass.

At the time in my life when things were beginning to

go well for my husband and me as a couple, I still had goals that I wanted to accomplish as an individual. In spite of my circumstances, I never doubted that living out my dreams beyond the relationship was part of the plan for me. We should be able to be ourselves in the relationship, and because I am now married, I believe that being with my husband should enhance my life, not take from it. I was blessed with the opportunity to express myself to the world through my first book, and I brought my husband along with me on this journey instead of leaving him out. In fact, we did the book together. Although this book was my dream, he was very much a part of it. If you are in a relationship and you have dreams that you have yet to live out, see how it might enhance your life to include your partner versus trying to live your dream with them on the sideline.

My husband and I were given the support we needed to pursue the life that we had dreamt of together. To me, this was the life that we were meant to live. We both wanted to make a difference in the world. We both wanted to continue to help others by being examples, serving as living proof, and by doing what we could to be supportive of other people's goals. We encouraged others in our everyday lives, and we were met with the challenges that inevitably came our way. Life was meant to be lived with joy and abundance, and we understood that, or at least that was my understanding. Remember that your husband could have a very different perception than you do. It's almost like growing up in the same household with a sibling and having completely different perceptions on how you were both raised — it happens.

I was doing my best to stay strong and faithful in life and in love. My husband and I were doing well in business, and we were in pursuit of lifelong happiness together. Once in a relationship though, there are always many challenges. Some may be avoided with discussion about each other's feelings and mutual respect, but life happens and nothing prevents issues from arising, whether you are in a weak relationship or in a strong and healthy one. Family and/or friends may become an issue. Money may become an issue. Sex may become an issue. Personal time versus work time, infidelity, drugs or alcohol may all become issues in a relationship, and the list goes on and on. Statistics say that every marriage will experience either adultery, addiction, or abuse. Are you and your partner ready to face any of those obstacles to a committed relationship? I was not, and I am still not, but that doesn't shield my husband and me from problems. I don't think that anyone is ever ready for these very difficult relationship challenges, but how a couple deals with them will determine whether or not they stay together. Dr. Martin Luther King Jr. said, "The ultimate measure of a man is not where he stands in moments of comfort and convenience, but where he stands at times of challenge and controversy." I'd say that this truth should also be applied to relationships, and applied equally to both men and women. Personally, I haven't been up for all of the challenges that have come my way, but the impact would not be the same if we knew which challenges we'd be faced with or when they were coming, would it? Half the battle would be won. Just know that you WILL BE TESTED.

Another challenge that will inevitably come up in serious relationships is childhood issues. Have you or your partner really gotten past them? These issues are usually what leads to the greater issues at hand. I heard a television pastor say that "hurt people hurt people," and I was struck by this very simple yet profound statement. What things did you not get to say to someone who hurt you when you were a child? Who disappointed you? Who disrespected you or someone you loved? Who abandoned you? Every one of us has experienced something that we were not happy with as a child, but who has yet to get past it? Be careful not to allow these hurt feelings to rob you of a happy marriage and future, to keep you from accepting your partner's love. This could happen consciously or subconsciously, so please be aware.

REAL TALK 14

I do not have all of the answers, but because I know where your heart is, I'm trying to remind you that, in the world of relationships, it's never just about you: your side, your viewpoint, your perception. Work on you while you only have you to worry about, because once you make the commitment to share your life with another person, your focus will change. You will need enough faith and love to weather the storms before you receive the blessings that come once you reach that understanding. I want love and happiness for you, but it's no easy task.

CHAPTER FIFTEEN
Have Enough to Give

Business was going well enough that my husband and I thought that we should take the time to come up with a plan to begin our next business venture. We were used to being blessed with these wonderful opportunities to grow whether or not there was a financial reward. At the very least, we would have another experience under our belts and we would know that we tried. Prior to actually making the final purchase of our biggest venture to date, however, we would run across yet another exciting business opportunity. Before it was all over, we ended up with four businesses and the blessings continued, or were the greatest challenges of our lives yet to come?

Just five short months earlier, we received the greatest gift any married couple could receive, a beautiful baby boy. No frozen eggs, no extra changes, just God's plans for us. After the many victories, including the most frightening, the cancer, we were blessed to have a child of our own. We had looked forward to this, but we knew that it was only through God's grace that we would see that day. The time that it took for God to prepare him was fun-filled and exciting. I remember thinking that we were the perfect couple for this to happen through. We were both celebrating our 30th birthdays, and we had been together for several years now, completely by choice. We had grown through very challenging young adult times during college and after, and we were spiritually connected, financially stable, and at a very comfortable place in our lives together. They say that hindsight is 20/20, and looking back, I wished that we would have spent more time focusing on the blessing of being able to raise our new son by taking our time instead of moving so fast to press on to the next big thing. It has been said never to leave one blessing looking for another, and I can attest to the truth of that. We were now trying to make a brighter future at a faster pace because we had a child. We wanted to put ourselves in a good enough position financially that we could spend as much time as we wanted with our son.

God was still working on us both independently and as a team. We had tried many different things over the years in business and education, but what seemed the most logical and perfect next step in life hadn't turned out the way we envisioned when we sat down with the idea. I am a big dreamer, and so of course I imagined that all of the success would come our way. I imagined that we would meet Oprah and other people who have inspired us, and that perhaps we'd be introduced to our next great idea. I have not let go of the dream today, but I have loosened up around the exact time that things are supposed to happen according to my plan. I told you that God has a plan that will prevail in each of our lives. After writing my first book, which He knew I needed to be able to do and at that time, God wanted something else to happen for my husband and me. He wanted to put us through more tests together and individually, even if we didn't understand that then.

Struggling to find balance with all that was going on personally and in business for us, I found myself praying that God would keep our relationship, our family, strong. If there were to be a breakdown in the partnership between my husband and me, the family would suffer, and so prayer is warranted in just the right order. I believe that it is necessary to pray for us, the married couple, and then for our children, because without being strong as individuals and as a team, what can we give to them? They need us. I know that some will disagree with me, but it's like getting on the airplane and they tell you that in the event of an emergency you should place the oxygen mask on yourself first and then assist the child next to you. Our children are depending on us, and we owe it to them to be strong. Another very important detail in relationships, speaking of children, is being loved for who you are and what you bring to the relationship, not for the sake of the kids. Please note that no one stays in a relationship just for the children, so don't buy that if someone has given you this excuse. I don't deny that, in many cases, the children will obviously have something to do with the relationship going forward, but it's never just "for" the kids. Everyone suffers in the end if the love isn't sincere.

Over the course of the next several months, a few of my family members came to stay with us for various reasons. The primary reason for the first guest was to help us with our son while we were trying to get back to work and some degree of normalcy, at least for me. We didn't feel comfortable with outsiders taking care of our son yet, and so my sister was the first to offer to come and help. You see, although I awaited the arrival of my son and was delighted at being honored in this way, I had never had a child before and so the compromise for me as a new mother was challenging. I wasn't comfortable enough in my ability to do well all the things that I needed to do as a mom. Balance took on a new meaning, and I am still working to be my best example of that.

Wouldn't you know it however, as soon as we were comfortable enough with the support we had for our primary business, my sister to help with the baby, the move that would allow us to expand and grow, we would receive a major blow. Our team player, the person we relied on the most for support with our company, gave us two-weeks notice. We were devastated. We now had two new businesses, two existing businesses, and no real help. We also had a baby boy and my sister, who also had a son, at home with us. We got a few more visitors, my family members, which turned into support for the business while we were trying to pull things together. Though this seemed like a good idea at the time, remember I mentioned that family may bring about issues in your relationship. The thing about family is that you love them so their problems weigh on you and can become your problems, and what becomes your problem also becomes the problem of your spouse. It's not so easy to take on your spouse's family members' problems because it may be something that you do not understand or agree with. For your own family though, not only do you care about the outcome of their problems but many times you were there for the onset (like early on in childhood) so their problems are a lot harder to ignore. It might be a lot to ask of your spouse so remember that fact.

Looking back, it was good that a few of my family members got to be there at the same time and perhaps work through some of the feelings that they needed to resolve with each other. I also knew that my own relationships were being challenged, and I knew that, as my husband and I were receiving help, we were giving it. I felt it was something we could get through, and I believed that my husband agreed.

Although I did say my relationships (plural) were being challenged because I needed to work through some feelings, like those with my father, who was also visiting at the time, the one relationship that always has to be strong when you are helping others is the one between you and your spouse. You and your spouse work together as a team, and therefore help for others comes from both of you, which may be hard for family to accept or understand. The two of you have to agree that the space is available in your marriage to deal with someone else's problems or your problems with someone else. Your marriage has to have enough to give. We certainly had more than enough on our plates emotionally, but like many couples, I think we pushed it to the limit, placing the difficulty of all that we were going through on the back burner as we tried to help others.

Everyone who came to our home played a role in our business or our home life to some degree, and I hope that we were able to help them. However, never did I take into consideration how much the loss of the energy being put into our own relationship could hurt my husband and me. I struggled through many nights, just being frustrated about the decisions that a few of them were making for themselves, the difficulty associated with getting a major business off of the ground, the pressure that my husband and I were now under with our time, businesses, and finances only to have God say, "Hey, I got a surprise. You are pregnant." I now knew why I was even more tired than I should be having an infant and getting very limited sleep.

Family, by virtue of the very nature of the love that you share together, can make any relationship extremely tough. All of us came from a family prior to getting together with someone who will become your family. Our biological families don't always know how to treat us differently than they did when we were just a single person, which may cause problems for our partners in fact, especially if our choice for a partner isn't all that family oriented and we are. Perhaps they don't understand or had a really negative experience with their own family. It is important that you find a compromise as a couple and take each other's feelings into very serious consideration when you refer to each other's family. My husband and I love each other's families, but we struggle in this area as many couples do. Part of this struggle for us is a cultural one because many Black families in America are close with extended family members and are expected to help out those who aren't doing so well, and regardless of how little the person may be doing for themselves. These challenges may be ongoing, a continual struggle throughout your relationship, so talk about your expectations and how you will address your families' respective expectations together. A word of advice: Treat your partner's feelings as you would have them treat yours, and really try to be honest so that you don't resent anyone, especially your partner, over the long haul.

REAL TALK 15

I want to repeat two things here: Before trying to help anyone else with their problems, agree that the space is available in your relationship, that your own marriage has enough to give because that energy comes from the two of you when you are connected the way that God connects you. Remember that your relationship, the health of the whole relationship, comes first, before anything else, even the children. Take care of each other and your marriage, and your children will benefit.

CHAPTER SIXTEEN

Forgive But Never Forget

Each one of us should understand that, until we are blessed with another person to love and support in life, we must learn to love ourselves. We've heard this all before, but we teach others how to treat us by what we allow people to get away with in their behavior toward us. Keep in mind that past behavior is the best predictor of future behavior, and while you can't make another person do anything, you don't have to accept being mistreated by anyone. We sometimes teach others what works for us by the way we treat other people. We show them what is acceptable and unacceptable. Ideas about the things that are okay versus those things that are not should be given careful thought and consideration. The things that I am most proud of about myself during my early relationships include pursuing my educational and career goals despite the mess my relationships were in. I always knew that I would be of more value to myself as well as to another person with the knowledge and experience gained through my personal trials.

I encourage each of you to get to know yourselves,

your likes and your dislikes, so that you don't have to put on a façade when confronted by someone else's interests. It's easy to fall in line and agree with another to avoid being too difficult, but it's not easy to continue living this way when you realize that you have lost who you are. Try new things. Start over. Don't be afraid to step out on faith when all you have to rely on is you. It will be a great test of your will, your strength, and your faith.

In *I Want It Now!*, I focused on the idea that each of us should dream and pursue our own happiness. The underlying message of that book is one that I still believe today, and if I were to add anything, I would reiterate that it usually takes a lot of hard work to see things through to fruition. You never know how the cards will be dealt to you, but you have to spend your life creating options for yourself, and you have to be as happy as possible in the place where you are during these times. Often, it's hard to imagine that we go through difficulties for a reason that actually makes us stronger in the long run, but always remember that you are not the only one. So many in this world suffer at the hands of others, or worse, they suffer over something they themselves control.

Don't give in to negativity because something seems unfair. God may just be preparing you for the many blessings that he has in store for you later. We learn about ourselves through life's many complexities. For example, my first book wasn't the best book in the world, but I loved it. It was written with my sincerest compassion for life and love. I got a message out in a way that I had never thought I would. It was amazing to turn my dream into reality. I was blessed to go across the country and speak to people about my life experiences, spreading a little hope and encouragement, a little sunshine to others who may not have understood their own purpose in life, to people who needed to hear this message. I met some interesting people. I shared messages of faith. I grew as an individual, which confirmed for me that God was real. What can be better than that? Have all of my life lessons been learned? Of course not, but I know that I am on my way.

Obviously, there are ups and downs for couples just as there are for individuals. However, it seems as though the bad times have gotten worse but the good times have also gotten better as I have grown older. This is only my experience, so don't be afraid. However, it is important to note that I have been trying to place my finger on how long these times of both kinds last. Don't get me wrong: I don't spend the good times waiting for the bad times to happen. The point is that I know that the bad times are coming and it is very important to be in the moment, just as I believe in my heart without question that the bad times will come to an end. I suggest that you become aware when a positive change begins to happen in your life. As with all good things, it will be up for a while but it will eventually top out, and while things are going well, it is important to prepare so that you can be strong enough to withstand the tough times. That is, prepare while things are up in your relationship for the many obstacles that will come your way when things are looking down. Ride the highs and endure the lows, for one thing that I always know is that I am being taught something about myself, my life, or my relationship each time things are down. If you analyze your own trials, you may find a similar pattern.

You may be wondering why so much of this book is about personal challenges that I've faced along with those faced by my husband. I do not think that the topic of love and relationships can be addressed without talking about the people that make them up. I also believe that many of us are afraid of sharing our truths because it can be so painful, but it's also during these times that we grow the most and can then truly help others. My husband and I had to grow as individuals in order to be a strong team, a worthy couple, but we are still growing. I believe in love and I believe that, with it, the world is a better place. Each of us is happier. Love doesn't come easy, but you sometimes have to go along for the ride when you are being led by a Higher Source.

Remember: to get yourself prepared for a true love relationship, you must get comfortable with yourself. Dream a little. Know what you want so that you are able to share that with someone else. Understand why you are who you are so that you know the best ways to address things about yourself that you are not so satisfied with. Define happiness for yourself, and determine what will be acceptable in a relationship. There is so much work for you to do in the meantime.

A holistic approach is needed when it comes to working on yourself until that true love and relationship comes along. In short, get your spiritual and physical health in order. Find balance in your life with work and education, or even more so, social activities. Discover those things that you are passionate about and want to work toward in your life, whether or not you have a man in it. So many women are waiting around for that miracle man to land in their laps, being lonely, sad and depressed, or even bitter in the meantime. Again I say, there is so much work to do so get busy. As Rev Run says, "A human being has no discernible character until he acts.... You cannot build a reputation on what you intend to do!" This applies to relationships as well. Get to work on you and he will come along. You will find that, because you have been so busy, it did not seem so long after all. Nurture the friendships and relationships that are important to you now so that you know the ones that you need to continue to support once you are in a relationship with a man.

Trust is a very important factor in a love relationship. You and your partner should be able to trust each other to look out for the best interests of the whole before thinking of the individual. This leads me to the very important topic of money. If you can't trust each other enough to have joint money with your spouse, you've got major issues to work out. The way couples deal with money has a lot to do with how each was raised, so think back. If your current money strategy as a couple didn't work for your parents, it probably will not work for you. Ask them about it.

One partner is probably better at keeping things in financial order than the other, but whatever you do, come to some sort of an agreement that you are going to work together for the good of the whole, your family. Have a joint bank account but have individual accounts too. Your spouse shouldn't necessarily know that you are buying them a gift or planning a surprise getaway. Be sure to compromise about the significance of money in your relationship, how much money you and your partner want to have, and how you will get it. We have all heard that money is the primary reason for divorce, so consider yourself warned. Don't lose love over finances. Learn about money and be smart about it so that you and your spouse can enjoy the many luxuries that money can buy together. Remember that money is not the root of evil, but the love of money is. So love your spouse first, love your family and let money be a tool to live abundantly and enjoy all that life has to offer.

There are many signs that a relationship is unhealthy or not likely to work, but we don't always see the signs — and perhaps we don't want to see them. I remember being so into certain guys based on who I thought the guy could be, based on his potential. Remember, his potential is not who he is. Everyone has potential. I mentioned that infidelity, drugs, or abuse may become issues in relationships — these are the widely known red flags. Although we all know that women as well as men cheat on their spouses (and women at rising rates), I am addressing the more common of the two because there will likely be more women reading this book than men. When he cheats he appears to be just spending more time out of the home, perhaps hanging out with "friends" or spending more time at the office after work hours. However, he is also more concerned about his physical appearance, maybe even buying new things here and there. He is not as concerned about your feelings and there will likely be a change in your sex life and financial picture. Perhaps there are changes with the money because likely he has money that is now a secret, used to support his infidelity. I liken infidelity to drugs because both situations entail a breakdown in communication, lies, unaccounted for time, changes with money and a distance that didn't seem to exist before. Trust me that a breakdown of this sort can happen in any relationship, a weak one or a strong one, and not just in the type of men that we imagine when we think of cheaters.

Chris Rock has a movie called *I Think I Love My Wife* that displays a very realistic approach to this issue. If I have said nothing else of significance to you in this book, know that this can happen to you in your relationship; and if it does, remember that it does not reflect on who YOU are. Work on yourself so that you will be able to listen to what God wishes for you should you ever be confronted by something so difficult and so serious.

I've heard it said that anything that people get divorced for, they could forgive someone for, and statistics say that 70% of all marriages have experienced adultery. The very thought is so scary to me because it means that there are lots of hurt feelings and dishonest communication about our true needs in relationships. Many people are feeling alone and afraid even in their marriages, wherein they have committed themselves to another person. I believe that, when this happens, there has obviously been a breakdown in the spirit, verbally or even emotionally, and it makes me sad for the person who feels that they need to go outside of their marriage for a temporary resolution that will ultimately make things much worse. However, I believe that two people can get past infidelity if they decide to communicate more effectively and work together with God on strengthening themselves individually and as a couple. This is such a major concern to me because I know that there are so many women out there suffering from low self esteem or who are willing to settle for less than what they should have. I wrote this book in part for those women, and a change in these women's well-being will in turn be good for all women. After all, the adulterers are cheating with someone.

I mentioned earlier that "hurt people hurt people," so if your spouse hurts you in this manner, it is likely more a product of their own problem than it is you. There are so many books out there on this topic that address why someone might cheat or even do drugs or drink alcohol excessively, but my goal is to help you to be strong as an individual so that you can contribute to your relationship rather than merely take from it. Know that you can get through any situation that exists in a relationship with your partner if that is something that the both of you want for yourselves, but the two of you must have a spiritual guide because you cannot overcome life's many tragedies alone. It will not be easy because it takes a lot for two people to work together, regain trust, and get through things they don't necessarily understand — faith is necessary in a relationship just as love and trust are. I know it's hard, but God is love and with Him a way can be made.

To the many women out there who are hurting and believe they will never find anyone to give them the love they deserve, I say, don't lose faith in love. As I have said

FORGIVE BUT NEVER FORGET

before, God may just be trying to strengthen your love for *you* because He knows of the many challenges that you are going to face in your relationship. Trust that God loves you and that He is preparing you, testing you even. Do your best not to wear that pain on your sleeve because there will always be those out there waiting to manipulate you into giving them what they want, which compromises who you are. Some men will be waiting to exploit your weakness, which in many cases is the fact that you are lonely and don't have a man in your life and want one so badly. Such a man will soothe your immediate pain if you let him, but he'll rip out a little more of your heart eventually once you get all caught up and he returns to his wife or moves on to the next vulnerable woman, leaving you worse than how he found you. My husband shared with me that, if a woman cheats with you, she'll cheat on you. Do you think a man wants you when you have contributed to his ultimate disappointment in himself by making it so easy not to address his real problems? Don't allow your pain from a failed relationship to convince you that you are undeserving of love and therefore other women who are in a relationship don't deserve to be happy either. You should never settle for a piece of a man because you don't think you deserve love.

Consider all of the players in a game like this. For example, the wife, who in many cases is unsuspecting. Sometimes, she may be aware of the kind of man she married, and maybe she feels defeated in this journey with him. Other times, however, a wife may never imagine her husband as a cheater. Never forget that, while you are eventually hoping to become a permanent part of this man's life, you are extremely vulnerable, calling this same infidelity into your own life later on down the line when you think your relationship is working out. Karma is real, especially when you know you are wrong but turn a blind eye. Also consider the children, if there are any, and I mean yours and his. What kind of example are you setting for your child by allowing yourself to be second best, hopefully getting in a phone call on the holidays and a few hours on some evenings when he is supposed to be somewhere else. I cannot believe that any woman is truly okay with being in that position, unless she too is married or has a boyfriend and that is a whole different can of worms. His children, who are robbed of a man at his best, should be considered because, if he is giving his time to you and his wife, he is missing out on life's most precious and intangible gifts, which includes being a whole man who is strong in his convictions and true to himself. The man himself should also be considered, because he may very well eventually despise you for participating in this game with him, despise you for being so weak that you didn't require him to be more. He will blame you for it later. How often does the woman who cheats with a married man end up with him? Less than 5% of the time, according to studies. So consider the entire scope of this situation and don't sketch out a future that you don't want to live.

For the wife and family, an act like cheating is horrible. I have witnessed the devastation that infidelity causes from the time I was a little girl. I saw it all around me, and it was almost a given that I would continue to see the results of this type of reckless behavior in my adult life.

There are enough men out there, and God will bless you with the one He wants you to have when He thinks that you are ready. Have faith. If you allow yourself to be misused by a man, take responsibility for not having enough faith in love or belief in yourself, which equates to not having enough faith in God. Renew your spirit. Ask God to forgive you for not loving you. And open your heart to God. He will provide for you. My mission statement in life is to Dream Big; Open Your Heart; Always Have Faith; And Follow Your Spirit Toward Ultimate Happiness. I wish this for each of you, and I continue to believe in this for myself through the many challenges that life and love have brought me. I know that I have more to learn, and therefore, more difficult times will come — I am sure of it.

It's always so easy to speak of our experiences while we are no longer staring them in the face, and it is easy to tell another person what's best for them. Would you rather hear someone tell you to keep allowing someone to hurt you because it feels good right now? If someone does say this to you, don't blame them because they obviously don't know the truth, or perhaps they are hurting themselves. Testimony is respectable. Could I have put this same information into a book to perhaps help someone else who might have been going through the same thing while I was going through it? Probably not. I have sat down and tried many times to think about the place where certain experiences fit into my life. I was unable to wrap my thoughts around the reasons that certain situations were becoming my own much less find the energy to speak about them.

Like many of you, I have gone through things in relationships that I never should have allowed to happen to me. I did not cause these things to happen to me, but my response dictated whether they would happen again. I cannot tell you today why I did not handle the situations differently or make better decisions, but I have had to live with the choices that I made. I have had to accept the good along with the bad, and I have moved on each time. Don't get me wrong. I am still a work in progress in many areas of my life and of my relationship. Why don't our hearts listen to our minds? If I knew the answer to that question, there would be no need for books like this. In love, just because we know better doesn't mean that we will do better. Begin to do better and your relationships will become better.

Let me just add again that cheating is a two-way street, but I directed this encouragement to the women versus the men because I don't share in a male's perspective about why he may cheat. Although I wish love and happiness for all, including both the men and the women, I am speaking to the daughters of men who cheat, the wives of men who cheat, and the women who cheat with these men because I understand more closely who you are. While I seek understanding for the many women confronted by this immense pain, I am praying for the men who need better examples, guidance, spiritual growth and healing while they place more value on the intangibles of life. Some things are worth standing up for.

REAL TALK 16

You can't love God and not love yourself. They are really one in the same. Love doesn't work without faith. Love is manifested via the spirit, so pay attention and you'll find out all you want to know. Require the God that is in you to be treated better, and you won't allow people to treat you badly. Remember that another person's shortcomings don't have to reflect who you are or who you have to be. To those of you who will continue to be the other woman, often referred to as the "clean up woman," note that there ain't no future in "cleaning up." Sometimes you have to stand up and do what is best for you, even when it hurts. Only love can hurt that good.

CHAPTER SEVENTEEN
You Don't Know Me

When I was younger, I remember my father making the comment, "If you wait until you get to know everything there is to know about a person before you marry them, you won't get married." I don't recall him seriously advising me in this way, and in fact, he chuckled a bit after he said it, but I could tell that he was quite serious. I didn't understand it then, but my understanding has since evolved and I am very clear.

My mother and father were never officially married. They were together for 22 years until it was over. It was unfortunate for both of them that they sold themselves short. I remember hearing someone say that my mother could have gotten my dad to marry her if she wanted to be married, but I'm not sure where her heart was around that particular issue. She loved my dad immensely, and he loved her for sure, but they had eventually gotten to a point in their relationship where love alone wasn't enough to sustain it. I never doubted that she wanted to be his wife, but with the kind of problems that they encountered, I can honestly say now that I can understand her being somewhat hesitant. However, I don't think that she believed in herself enough. My father, though a great guy, really didn't allow himself to be the man he could have been, a man like his own father. Perhaps he didn't believe in himself enough to be ready to approach his own greatness either. Fear is very powerful.

The longer one waits to make a commitment like marriage, the more reasons one will come up with for why it might not be such a good idea and the less likely one will be to make the final commitment. So let's explore the topic of getting to know your partner. So often in relationships, we are around other people without truly knowing who they are and many times we don't even know ourselves as well as we think we do. This is so because we learn more about ourselves and others based on our responses or reactions to circumstances and situations. Usually, the most difficult situations are the ones that teach us the most. I read once that three of the elements that really make a man or a woman include hard work, sincerity, and commitment; but none of these things are given lightly. In fact, these three things are all intertwined and speak to the core of who a person really is. If you truly know someone, you will have seen these items beat out fear. These are also things that you have to see in action to believe.

There is no way to get to know everything there is to know about a person because we are all ever evolving. We each have different experiences that shape who we are and how we see things, but I encourage you to go through as much as you can with the person you are considering for a partner. Spend as much time as you can getting to know each other, and in particular getting to know each other's pasts and feelings about the past. Find out about the men and women who played a part in the upbringing of your potential mate, and find out how they feel about them or the decisions they made. These people have inevitably had an impact one way or the other on them. Watch how your significant other treats people or responds in difficult circumstances outside of the relationship. They are showing you who they really are. We've all heard the saying, believe a person when they *show* you who they really are; but so often, our own view becomes clouded by what we don't think they would do to *us* that we see what we want to see instead of exactly who they are showing us. Eventually we become old and comfortable instead of fresh and new, and we are no longer someone to be excited about or to "put on the new shoes for." Boundaries may begin to get crossed because times may become more difficult. Ever see someone have a completely cynical attitude about life and the world around them but they are excited about love and relationships? Probably not, so pay attention to the signs.

What do you do when you find out that the person that you have chosen to share your life with isn't who you thought they were? This sad reality is one of the most devastating experiences. It feels like betrayal, but is this betrayal when that person has been showing you all along but you refused to see them for who they were? For example, if he never likes to follow rules or stay within boundaries, how can you be surprised when he cheats on you. Who is responsible then? I know that perhaps you didn't see his infidelity coming, but it may very well have been there all along. What happens when your significant other exposes something about himself, shows his true colors, that you had not noticed before, something that you don't like because you yourself are now looking through different eyes? Who is responsible for the changes that will then be necessary? Mature and committed adults understand that both people in a relationship need to be willing to do the work to adjust to the growth and change. It is all a part of growing up and becoming a better person.

Men and women do not think the same. Sometimes, the gift of another person's weakness could be your blessing. You never know what God is trying to teach you or your significant other. It could simply be that you need to grow, or it could be that your significant other is not growing. Either way, it is best to know who you have in your life. This will tell you what you can accomplish together, what you can achieve. Finding out early enough can prevent you from waking up one day next to someone you don't respect or value, or even someone you resent or despise. Regardless of what you find out though, we can only control ourselves in a relationship. Knowing yourself could also help you to prevent a relationship disaster. If you discover one day that you have married someone that you do not know, or perhaps someone that you have grown apart from, the commitment that you made to one another before God should be reason enough to make the effort to work through the adjustment phase. Both people in the relationship have to be willing, and most importantly, both people have to recognize that God is the strength that the two of you need. If you are not married yet, make a good choice so you won't have to regret it.

REAL TALK 17

Now, don't get mad because this one may not be for everybody. Sometimes people buy into the following notion: if it ain't broke, don't fix it; and if it don't fit, don't force it. But if you are in a relationship with someone who will not honor you with a commitment before God, allowing you to receive His blessing on your union together, your relationship is broken. Not everyone in a relationship desires marriage, which is okay, but if you are living as married people do and if you have children together, perhaps you should consider whether your fears are stopping you from reaching your individual greatness. Don't be afraid, and this is not judgment. The rules were written — and I didn't write them — so if you want to be married, ask God's blessing with moving you forward within and apart from your significant other.

CHAPTER EIGHTEEN
In the Meantime

I know that you want to be told what you could be doing while you are waiting for your Prince Charming, or perhaps even what to do to find him. My advice is to find YOU. Before you open yourself up to share your life with another person, find out who you are and what you really want in your life. Figure out what you need. Develop your character, your vision, your philosophy. Read some good books. Take a few trips. Develop your important friendships and family bonds. Take advantage of opportunities to explore your career goals and options, and learn about things that are of importance to you. Give back in areas where you have been blessed abundantly, whether financially, creatively, or otherwise. Join an organization where you will meet positive and supportive people. Network. Go to church or find a place of spiritual solitude. Get comfortable in your skin and in your body. Listen to your spirit so that you can grow in your spirituality. When your heart and spirit are working together and are in the right place, God knows it, and He will provide you with what you need and with what you are ready for.

I know that this is hard to hear, but not every relationship is meant to be. Not every cute guy is worthy of your time. I remember wanting a certain guy to like me back, to desire me as I desired to have him. I remember giving so much in a relationship with young men who were taking from me. I remember questioning who I was because I had gotten myself involved in one bad situation after another with guys. Some women are always referring to how long they have been together or involved with someone, and they think that should be reason enough for this to be the right relationship. When it comes down to it, in many cases, all we end up with in some relationships is time. Just because we have been involved for a long period doesn't mean that there has been any growth, individually or for the couple. If there is no growth, there is no life. Are you in a dead relationship? If yes, get out while you are ahead, while you still have the chance. Get out before you are married to that dead relationship and have no more fight left in you to be all that you can be. In college, I remember hearing, "Rejection is God's gift of protection." I embraced that as best I could. If I can give any advice to those young women wondering why they keep getting rejected by the man they think could be "the one," it is this: keep in mind that he could just be the one to remind you that God doesn't see him fitting into your life. Trust me, God knows what He's doing even when you think you know better. Remember that God also knows the man in question.

Think about purpose in your relationships. Some peoples' purpose in our relationships is to remind us of who we want to be, and others serve to show us who we are. If you don't like what you see, what will you do about it? What are you willing to change? I know that it is always easier to tell someone to leave a bad situation than it is to actually do it. It's easier for all of us. Many of us are in long-term relationships. Many are married or divorced, afraid of being alone perhaps. Many have children, and I never suggest ending a relationship with your spouse or breaking up your family. I just want to encourage you all to consider those important things before the situation gets to be much more complicated than just walking away from a bad situation.

One of the primary reasons I needed to write this book was because I know that love and relationship issues are REAL. I know the pain is REAL, and I know that the love itself is REAL. I know that to be happy in our lives is why we are all here. I know that there is much too much to enjoy in this life to spend so much time down or afraid. Don't be. Always know that God is working on you and that He knows what you need. Develop a mission statement in your life, one that reflects who you are and what you believe. I know that many of you are in relationships that are working, and I only wish continued happiness for you. I encourage you to try to be supportive and an example to someone who aspires to be in a solid and blossoming relationship as well. Be as honest as possible in sharing your situations so that they may truly grow from your experience. Love others and be truthful as you should also love *you* and be truthful to *yourself*. Be sure that you share those things that you know work in relationships versus the things that don't so that more realistic pictures of relationships begin to exist for the public. I have put together a few things that I believe work, and although they are sometimes small, these suggested actions can be a really big deal. There is always work to do, so this list could really go on and on.

In a relationship, you should:

1. Be honest about your feelings
2. Talk about your concerns
3. *Not* keep major secrets
4. Explore your faith together
5. Combine your incomes into one main account
6. Confront your fears
7. Never exploit each other's weaknesses
8. Be spontaneous sometimes
9. Trust each other
10. Be yourself
11. Share each other's dreams
12. Explore each other's interests
13. Shop for each other
14. Get to know each other's likes and dislikes
15. Go out on dates
16. Find ways to uplift your partner
17. Entertain each other's friends or loved ones
18. Be a part of each other's family
19. Respect each other's opinions
20. *Not* take your arguments too seriously

21. Go on vacations together
22. Plan romantic evenings
23. Tell the other what they mean to you
24. Look at each other sometimes without talking
25. Step outside of your relationship sometimes in order to appreciate it

26. Hold hands in public
27. Support each other in accomplishing your goals
28. Dance or listen to music together
29. Never let anyone interfere
30. Seek to learn new things together

31. Encourage change and growth or improvement
32. Do things that are new for both of you
33. Go places together like the movies or museums and discuss these venues
34. Appreciate each other
35. Kiss each other when coming and going

36. Hug and touch each other
37. Rub or massage each other
38. Share your disappointments
39. Find the best method to discuss your problems
40. Be fair and compromising

41. Be committed to staying committed
42. Never say things that you might regret

43. Allow yourself to feel emotions and move past them
44. Share your expectations
45. Pay attention to your partner's needs
46. Pay attention to what your partner wants
47. Write notes, emails or letters to each other every now and then
48. Plan weekend getaways
49. Tell the other that you love them often
50. Eliminate divorce or break up from the options…so that together, you two can work it out!

And if you are married and/or have recently had children, because I am a new mother, I want to share with you that life will get better soon. It is tough in the beginning, and it's not until you are in this situation that you really understand this assertion. Find who you are underneath all of the extra layers of emotions and weight and stress and pressure you have put on since beginning this new journey. Your "You" is waiting to return to the scene, but you need to stay on top of your desire to return to, or become, the best you that you can be. Remember that your husband and your children need "You" to receive the blessing of a happy, healthy, and balanced wife and mom. Seek to regain or discover a new fire in you, a zest for life, and reach for your passion because you now have a couple of new eyes watching your every move. Good luck to you. You can do it.

REAL TALK 18

This section was by far the most difficult to write, and that is because "love" is the part of my life that I am currently living. It's hard to speak about something from the inside out. As with my first book, *I Want It Now!*, I am giving you the best of me, RIGHT NOW! My perception of love or my reasons for wanting to write this book may not be the same after a few years. As I shared before, I expect to do more growing because that is what life is about, which means there will indeed be changes, more experience, and I hope, more insight. I expect to grow with my husband as well. He and I are living day to day, facing new challenges as a couple, as parents, as entrepreneurs, as individuals. I am not trying to say that everyone should do as I have done, and in fact, I am saying that everyone should *find their own happiness* and be real about what their heart is telling them — what God is telling you. I know that He is speaking to your heart. Don't miss out by shutting him out. He knows where you have been and He knows what you've been through. He also knows what you can handle, but you have to stand up and do what you know you need to. STAND UP FOR YOURSELF. STAND UP FOR YOUR HEART. STAND UP FOR TRUE LOVE. Love is out there, and it doesn't have to hurt.

Love is but a portion bliss. The rest is challenge.
　　　—N. Crawford

Special Thanks

I want to say thank you to those men, young and old alike who have decided to do what was right, acknowledging the intangibles and not being led by the physical alone. Thank you to those men who care enough to stay, to those of you who have risen to the occasion of manhood. Thank you to those men who have chosen to do what was best for your families, your children even when you knew it would be easier to just do you. I want to thank those men who are not afraid to defy the odds, those who do what you feel in your heart regardless of what anyone else thinks because you know it's right. Thank you to those men who are proud of being supportive and involved fathers, to those men who respect women, themselves and each other. Thank you to those men who grow up and change bad patterns. Thank you to those men who will. Thanks to those men who respect the sanctity of marriage. I know that there are many of you out there and I just want to recognize you and say thank you. You are appreciated. I'm saying thank you to those men for us women who know that you exist.

My Mission Statement
Dream BIG; Open You Heart;
Always Have Faith; and Follow Your Spirit
Towards Ultimate Happiness!
—N. Crawford

For Speaking Engagements, Author Appearance or for more information on books or upcoming projects, please visit my website at
www.nakishacrawford.com or
call: 800-961-9431/fax 909-693-5363

For order information, please visit
www.sogoodithurts.com

To order *Real Talk Love* DVD,
please visit
www.realtalklove.com

Author

Na'Kisha Crawford is an accomplished and best selling Author, professional Life Coach and Inspirational Speaker and Entrepreneur whose goal is to inspire others to experience the journey. She has spoken to thousands of people from various backgrounds on topics that range from personal and professional growth to the development of healthy love and interpersonal relationships. Na'Kisha earned a Bachelor of Arts Degree in Sociology as well as a Master's Degree in Education, Counseling from San Jose State University.

Na'Kisha has taken on a variety of roles including being a panelist for principles that emphasized women in higher education and non-traditional professions as well as an expert life coach and national spokesperson for Downy Simple Pleasures on a campaign designed to improve the daily lives of working women. She has facilitated individual and group counseling sessions in addition to workshops on developing effective counseling techniques and she has conducted open forums for men and women on topics related to love and relationships. Na'Kisha has lectured collegiate level courses as well as written and implemented lesson plans for high school students on various subjects. These experiences have provided her with critical knowledge about the possibility of overall success in relationships and in life.

Na'Kisha is a licensed Real Estate Broker and she is also co-founder of a real estate investment and appraisal firm, serving as a corporate officer and CEO. She has consulted for small businesses and she, along with her husband, has started and operated several businesses of their own. Na'Kisha's creative energy and passion drive her to keep pushing forward to a healthy and balanced transition toward success.

Na'Kisha's debut book, "I Want It Now!" made critical acclaim and her sophomore project, So Good It Hurts, is sure to take the literary, non fiction world by storm with her new dose of "Real Talk" on love. She is confident that her professional, educational and real life experiences support her qualification. She was born a life coach and she has a strong interest in the personal development of her peers. Na'Kisha has a genuine desire to help people achieve success in life. She is a natural leader, she is experienced and she is passionate.

Just a few short years ago at age 27, Na'Kisha was diagnosed with Breast Cancer. She embraced this as one of the most challenging processes she would encounter but she was faithful that wonderful things were to come for her. She held her head up gracefully and accepted this challenge. Na'Kisha is now Cancer Free, wife and mother of 2 beautiful babies and she is sharing her passion with the world. She has an energy and an excitement that we cannot afford to miss.

Na'Kisha leaves you with this:

Something Like a Superwoman

"I am Something like a Superwoman.
I am a beloved wife and I have been chosen to be mother
of 2 beautiful babies as well as a stepmother.
I am a friend, a soror, and a sister.
I am Something like a Superwoman.
A National Best-Selling Author, a very passionate
motivational speaker, and an entrepreneur.
I am Something like a Superwoman.
Educated, an independent thinker, creative
and successful in my endeavors.
I am Something like a Superwoman.
I am a hard worker, dedicated to making positive changes,
a natural born leader and active in my community.
I am a Cancer Survivor, Blessed and Highly Favored, and
I, like many other women in the world,
am Something like a Superwoman."

—N. Crawford

A friend shared with me that "A woman who doesn't work will do anything to survive" and to that I say, do what you need to do to be happy with the woman behind your eyes."

—*N. Crawford*